DEMELE: "MAKING IT"

IMMIGRANT COMMUNITIES & ETHNIC MINORITIES IN THE UNITED STATES & CANADA: No. 70

ISSN 0749-5951

Series Editor: Robert J. Theodoratus
Department of Anthropology, Colorado State University

1. James G. Chadney. *The Sikhs of Vancouver.*
2. Paul Driben. *We Are Metis: The Ethnography of a Halfbreed Community in Northern Alberta.*
3. A. Michael Colfer. *Morality, Kindred, and Ethnic Boundary: A Study of the Oregon Old Believers.*
4. Nánciellen Davis. *Ethnicity and Ethnic Group Persistance in an Acadian Village in Maritime Canada.*
5. Juli Ellen Skansie. *Death Is for All: Death and Death-Related Beliefs of Rural Spanish-Americans.*
6. Robert Mark Kamen. *Growing Up Hasidic: Education and Socialization in the Bobover Hasidic Community.*
7. Liucija Baskauskas. *An Urban Enclave: Lithuanian Refugees in Los Angeles.*
8. Manuel Alers-Montalvo. *The Puerto Rican Migrants of New York City.*
9. Wayne Wheeler. *An Analysis of Social Change in a Swedish-Immigrant Community: The Case of Lindsborg, Kansas.*
10. Edwin B. Almirol. *Ethnic Identity and Social Negotiation: A Study of a Filipino Community in California.*
11. Stanford Neil Gerber. *Russkoya Celo: The Ethnography of a Russian-American Community.*
12. Peter Paul Jonitis. *The Acculturation of the Lithuanians of Chester, Pennsylvania.*
13. Irene Isabel Blea. *Bessemer: A Sociological Perspective of a Chicano Bario.*
14. Dorothy Ann Gilbert. *Recent Portuguese Immigrants to Fall River, Massachusetts: An Analysis of Relative Economic Success.*
15. Jeffrey Lynn Eighmy. *Mennonite Architecture: Diachronic Evidence for Rapid Diffusion in Rural Communities.*
16. Elizabeth Kathleen Briody. *Household Labor Patterns among Mexican Americans in South Texas: Buscando Trabajo Seguro.*
17. Karen L. S. Muir. *The Strongest Part of the Family: A Study of Lao Refugee Women in Columbus, Ohio.*
18. Judith A. Nagate. *Continuity and Change Among the Old Order Amish of Illinois.*
19. Mary G. Harris. *Cholas: Latino Girls and Gangs.*
20. Rebecca B. Aiken. *Montreal Chinese Property Ownership and Occupational Change, 1881—1981.*
21. Peter Vasiliadis. *Dangerous Truths: Interethnic Competition in a Northeastern Ontario Goldmining Center.*
22. Bruce La Brack. *The Sikhs of Northern California, 1904—1975: A Socio—Historical Study.*
23. Jenny K. Phillips. *Symbol, Myth, and Rhetoric: The Politics of Culture in an Armenian-American Population.*
24. Stacy G. H. Yap. *Gather Your Strength, Sisters: The Emerging Role of Chinese Women Community Workers.*
25. Phyllis Cancilla Martinelli. *Ethnicity In The Sunbelt: Italian-American Migrants in Scottsdale, Arizona.*
26. Dennis L. Nagi. *The Albanian-American Odyssey: A Pilot Study of the Albanian Community of Boston, Massachusetts.*
27. Shirley Ewart. *Cornish Mining Families of Grass Valley, California.*
28. Marilyn Preheim Rose. *On the Move: A Study of Migration and Ethnic Persistence among Mennonites from East Freeman, South Dakota.*
29. Richard H. Thompson. *Toronto's Chinatown: The Changing Social Organization of an Ethnic Community.*
30. Bernard Wong. *Patronage, Brokerage, Entrepreneurship and the Chinese Community of New York.*

Continued at back of book

DEMELE: "MAKING IT"

Migration and Adaptation Among Haitian Boat People in the United States

Rose-Marie Cassagnol Chierici

AMS Press, Inc.
New York

Library of Congress Cataloging-in-Publication Data

Chierici, Rose-Marie Cassagnol, 1942.
  Demele: "making it" : migration and adaptation among Haitian boat
people in the United States / by Rose-Marie Chierici.
  — (Immigrant communities & ethnic minorities in the United States
& Canada ; 70)
  Includes bibliographical references.
  ISBN 0-404-19480-X
  1. Haitian Americans—Social conditions. 2. Haitians—Foreign
countries—Social conditions. 3. Refugees, Political—United States—Social
conditions. 4. Haiti—Emigration and immigration. 5. Migration,
Internal—Haiti. I. Title. II. Series.
E184.H27C48 1991
305.8'9697294073—dc20   89-18506
                                                                          CIP

All AMS Books are printed on acid-free paper that meets the guidelines for performance and durability of the Committee on Production
Guidelines for Book Longevity of the Council on Library Resources.

AMS PRESS, INC.
56 East 13th Street
New York, N.Y. 10003, U.S.A.

Manufactured in the United States of America

WITHDRAWN

ACKNOWLEDGEMENTS

This book is a revised and updated version of my doctoral dissertation. Since the dissertation was written, in 1986, many changes have taken place, both in Haiti and in Haitian immigrant communities in the United States. I have tried to incorporate these changes in the book and to explain their importance for the two groups of Haitian immigrants I studied.

For their encouragement, criticism, and support, I would like to thank the members of the Department of Anthropology at the University of Rochester, in particular Dr. Alfred Harris, Dr. Grace Harris, and Dr. Anthony Carter. I owe special gratitude to Dr. Ayala Gabriel, my dissertation supervisor, for all the time we spent together discussing the data. I am very grateful to Dr. Michel Laguerre, of the University of California at Berkeley, for reviewing the manuscript, for his comments, and for his support. It meant a great deal to me. I wish to thank Dr. Theodore M. Brown, of the Department of History at the University of Rochester, and Dr. Sue Roark-Calnek, of SUNY Geneseo, with whom I have shared several exciting discussions.

I extend my profound gratitude to special friends: the members and staff of the BOCES Geneseo Migrant Center, in particular Dr. Gloria Mattera, Robert Lynch, Sylvia Kelly, and to Kathy Fox of the Cornell Migrant Program. In Rochester, the Catholic Family Center, Rural Opportunities, Inc. Paştor Brenton of Parsells Avenue Community Church, and Pastor Belcher of Community Bible Church provided assistance.

I also thank Karen Porter, for her editorial assistance, and Vicky Willis, of the Document Preparation Center at SUNY Brockport for preparing the manuscript. They were both patient, supportive, and cheerful.

I want in particular to thank those many informants who gave freely and cheerfully of their time, often after long hours in the field. This book is a tribute to their courage and determination.

I am finally most indebted to my husband who helped me go through the process of rediscovering my Haitian identity and ethnic pride. He planted the seed and patiently watched it grow. To my children, "Thank you for your patience."

TABLE OF CONTENTS

PREFACE

In the middle of the Winter of 1986, the Haitian people ended a long nightmare of political and social repression by a pacific mass rebellion against the almost three-decade long tyrannical and corrupt dynastic regime of Francois "Papa Doc" and Jean-Claude "Baby Doc" Duvalier, both of whom had ruled over the silent republic with an iron fist. It was also during this time that more than one million Haitian migrants left the island in search of political asylum or permanent residence status in various countries such as Venezuela, Mexico, the U.S. mainland and Puerto Rico, Jamaica, the Dominican Republic, Metropolitan France including French Guyana, Martinique and Guadeloupe, Zaire and elsewhere in Francophone Africa. Although much is said and known about the peculiar style of governance of the "tonton macoute" regime, the study of the impact of emigration on the transformation and reshaping of Haitian society, and of the adaptation of Haitian immigrants to the communities of their adopted country is still in embryonic form.

Recent internal and external Haitian migration
has functioned to defuse an otherwise explosive
situation. In previous decades, cities and villages
lost large portions of their populations, while at
the same time incorporating migrants from neighboring rural districts. As a result of rural-urban
migration, new squatter settlements have developed
in the periphery of the capital and secondary
cities. This constant flow of people has caused a
certain degradation of rural life, the feminization
of urban poverty, the housing crisis in the
metropolitan Port-au-Prince area, and the rise of
political consciousness among the proletariat.

While this demographic shift was taking place in
Haiti, Haitian immigrants in the United States were
busy developing their own communities. In major
American cities such as Miami, Chicago, Los Angeles,
Boston, and New York, Haitian immigrants have been
able to carve niches for themselves, while still
maintaining contacts with their homeland. This
situation is unique in Haitian history because it
marks the first time that upper and middle class individuals have emigrated in such large numbers.
Economic poverty alone does not adequately explain

this phenomenon; historically the country has always been poor, and poverty alone has never generated such a mass movement of illegal migration. Political repression was the additional ingredient - for some immigrants, it was the most critical factor forcing them to leave the island.

In some ways, Haitian immigrants to the United States have been like caged birds. This is largely because of the restrictive policies of the American government: on one hand, the government supported the oppressive and kleptomaniac administration of Jean-Claude Duvalier, and on the other hand, it refused to grant political asylum to the incoming refugees. For the most part, refugees were placed in jail-like detention centers, but some of them were deported back to the same repressive country from which they had fled. With the help of volunteer lawyers, local activists, and through the generosity of various humanitarian organizations, some refugees have been able to remain in their adopted country. It is the socio-economic adaptation of two segments of the refugee population who have migrated to upstate New York that Dr. Rose-Marie Chierici documents and analyzes in her book.

Dr. Chierici, who holds a Ph.D. in Social
Anthropology from the University of Rochester, has
carried out extensive field research among Haitian
refugees in two distinct environments: an urban setting - Rochester, New York; and a rural milieu - the
farm labor camps of upstate New York. These immigrants are "boat people"; people who were able to
reach the shores of Florida, and who later made a
second migration to the North. Her book is the
first major study available on internal migration of
Haitians in the United States.

Dr. Chierici places Haitian migration in a
center-periphery framework. Using the concepts of
cultural and social liminality, she is able to explain various phases of the adaptation process of
"boat people" to American society. Her account is
an interesting, informative, detailed, and accurate
ethnography of the movement of immigrants from Haiti
to Florida, and from there to upstate New York.
Particular attention is paid to the way the immigrants gathered the money needed to pay their passage, their strategies of acquiring a boat and
recruiting a pilot, their tribulations during the

"middle passage", their encounters with U.S. immigration agents, and the living conditions of their communities.

The book shows that ferrying refugees to Miami has become a lucrative business in several coastal communities in Haiti. The study also shows, however, that several individuals, especially those from adjacent islands such as Ile de la Gonave and Ile-a-Vache, have developed their own means to make the trip to the United States, using only frail sailboats and their skills. Needless to say, many of those refugees never visited the western portion of the island of Haiti. Since the central government has had a history of neglect vis-a-vis those island communities, one may predict that their inhabitants will continue to travel to the United States instead of migrating to the Haitian mainland, and that they may even someday seek greater political and administrative autonomy and control in managing their internal affairs.

Consistent throughout Dr. Chierici's findings is the energy and determination shown by the refugees to be self-sufficient, to do well in spite of adverse extraneous circumstances, and to continue to

financially assist family members in Haiti. The in-
genious and flexible strategies used by the immigrants to strengthen the economic basis of their
households and develop viable ethnic enclaves to
further their adaptation, to preserve their culture
and to provide emotional support are vividly spelled
out in Dr. Chierici's account.

The immigrants have already encountered many
difficulties. For some, however, the battle to
remain in the United States continues. Although
they were not welcomed by the U.S. government, the
Haitian "boat people" were supported by many legis-
lators and human rights advocates who lobbied for
the passage of the Immigration Act of 1986. This
act provides a legislative basis for the legalization of the status of refugees and illegal aliens in
the United States. Once the act became law,
however, the immigrants were subjected to one more
requirement; they had to prove that they did not
have acquired immuno-deficiency syndrome (AIDS).
Since AIDS is not a clearly defined disease, the
possibility exists that those individuals who test
positive for the syndrome did not import it, but acquired it in the detention centers in which they

were placed by U.S. law enforcers, such as Krome, Florida; Ray Brook, New York; and Fort Allen, Puerto Rico.

Another problematic aspect of the new immigration law concerns the philosophy and practice of family reunion, a central feature of traditional U.S. immigration policy. Under the new law, those individuals who arrived in the United States after January 1, 1982, are ineligible for immediate status adjustment. This, as well as the addition of immuno-deficiency syndrome carriers to the list of undesirable aliens, places another burden on immigrant communities. One of the immediate consequences of the latter stipulation, for example, is that the legal immigrant (or even the citizen), whose spouse or child is yet unapproved for legal residence, may himself (or herself) be barred from staying in the United States if his or her spouse does not meet the negative immuno-deficiency syndrome test requirement. The logic of such a policy, if carried to its ultimate end, will be an aberration, and is sure to cause more suffering to the less fortunate people of the land.

By allowing the people the opportunity to tell their stories, Dr. Chierici provides us with a very intimate portrait of the immigrants. Her research contributes immensely to our understanding of the history and functional adaptation of the "boat people" in the United States, and is an important contribution to the growing sociological literature on Caribbean migration. This well-researched book by a fine scholar should be required reading for all those involved in studying or working with Haitian immigrant communities throughout the United States.

                                    Michel S. Laguerre
                        University of California at Berkeley

CHAPTER I

INTRODUCTION

"Dèyè mòn gen mòn"
"Behind every mountain there is another mountain".

This Creole proverb reflects life as seen by Haitians: it is difficult to cultivate the hills, as there are so many of them in Haiti. To survive, Haitians must live with them and in spite of them.

As a metaphor, this proverb also means that problems, like mountains, are part of the Haitian horizon; they are always there. As one needs to cross mountains to go places, one has to resolve problems and go forward. It mirrors Haitians' *demele* attitude and positive outlook toward life. Goals are never final, and as one is reached, another comes into focus.

Demele is a Haitian Creole word that means to manage in the face of hardship, to make ends meet, to come up with a solution. Haitian immigrants use it frequently in their narratives to describe their experiences. *Demele* is central to the understanding of the strategies that Haitians use to "make it". In

1

this study, "making it" means, among other things, to
move from social periphery to center, and to migrate
from Haiti and adapt to American society. Migration
itself is *demele*; it is coming up with a solution, and
every strategy used in the process of adaptation is
permeated with *demele*, with "making it".

This book examines the migration and adaptation
processes of Haitian immigrants of rural and low income urban origins, who have entered the United States
illegally between 1978 and 1982. It investigates how
cultural ideas are used by Haitians in their choice to
migrate and in their everyday life in America, how
they affect their perceptions of Haitian and American
societies, and how they shape their expectations and
hopes for a better life in the United States.

This study places immigration within the context
of Haitian history and society. It emphasizes the importance of understanding historical and ecological
factors which have shaped Haitian society, including
its economic and political institutions. The historical perspective is used here to underline the
processes that shaped contemporary Haitian *conscience
collective*; in Durkheim's words, the "totality of

beliefs and sentiments common to the average citizens of the same society" (1933: 79).[1]

This study demonstrates how particular situations in the host society, such as the American class system and the legal status of the immigrants, affect the adaptation process and the range of adaptive strategies open to the immigrants. By adaptation, I mean the way individuals learn to function in a new culture and society. It is a process during which Haitian immigrants learn new rules of social behavior and become part of American society. This study also addresses the problem of ethnic identity and the importance of networks to Haitian immigrants.

Two segments of the Haitian immigrant population were studied for this project: migrant farm workers who come to Western New York in the fall for the potato harvest and immigrants who have settled in Rochester, New York. Members of both communities came to the United States at about the same time, between 1978 and 1982. They are part of the wave of migration commonly referred to as "boat people". Boat people entered the United States illegally via the Southern coast of Florida, having fled Haiti on small crafts.

MIGRATION AND ADAPTATION

The anthropological literature on migration and
adaptation is very extensive. In this book, I address
these issues within the narrower context of the
anthropology of the Caribbean Basin including Haiti.
In so doing, I place the present study on Haitian boat
people in the context of previous anthropological
studies on Haitian immigrants.[2]

I also include a brief review of some studies on
other migrant populations that have contributed to a
better understanding of the present discussion on
Haitians. Of particular interest to this project are
the works of Epstein (1958, 1964), Mitchell (1956,
1966, 1974), Parkin (1969), and Mayer (1964) on labor
migrations in Africa, and the meaning of "tribal"
identity in the process of migration from rural to urban areas. The analyses of Gluckman (1955), Mayer
(1961), Epstein (1981), and Mitchell (1966) are useful
in understanding the process by which ethnic identity
and ethnic boundaries are maintained in pluralistic
societies. The works of Bott (1971), Barnes (1954),
Mayer (1961), Mitchell (1969) point out the relevance

of network analysis as a way to describe migration and adaptation strategies within given sociocultural environments.

Other researchers have looked at the migration process and Haitian migration in particular.[3] A number of social scientists have examined the determinants and consequences of the "new Caribbean immigration" into the United States (Bryce-Laporte, 1976, 1977, 1978, 1979a, 1979b; Dominguez 1975; Safa and Dutoit 1975; Sutton 1973, 1975; Palmer 1976; Petersen 1958 and 1977; and Kritz 1981). There is agreement in the literature that new patterns of international migration have developed in the Caribbean Basin over the past thirty years, and that

> Immigration today is more a consequence and expression of the larger order or imbalance in national and international politico-economic relations than a reflection of simple increases in individual motivation, ordinary push-pull operations, or even increased accessibility to more capable transportation media. (Bryce-Laporte 1979a: 228).

Haitian migration

Several anthropologists have investigated the increased migration of Haitians to other Caribbean, North American, and European destinations. Bastide et al (1974) offered an overview of Haitian migration to several countries. Jean-Baptiste (1979), Smat (1973), Berardin-Haldeman (1972), Dejean (1978) have focused on Haitians living in Canada. There are several references in the literature to the migration of Haitian wage-laborers to neighboring countries and French overseas territories, such as the Dominican Republic (Bajeux 1980, Corten 1976, Diaz 1976, Duarte 1976, Fink 1979, Grasmuck 1982, Logan 1968), Cuba (Diaz 1973, Palmieri 1980), Guadeloupe (Hurbon 1982), French Guyana (Boggio 1982), and the Bahamas (Dominique 1982, Marshall 1979, 1982).

Allman (1982) offers a review of the literature on Haitian migration between 1950 and 1980, and concludes that "knowledge of current trends and their determinants remains fragmentary and incomplete" (p. 7). On the other hand, Perusek (1984) suggests that standard migration theory does not apply to the Haitian situation. He claims that conditions in Haiti, rather

than conditions in the host countries, seem to influence the rate of Haitian migration. Haitian migration, he suggests, has to be viewed in light of the
broader economic, social, and political context of the
Caribbean. I address these issues in Chapter II.

Likewise, Stepick (1984) claims that existing
models of migration cannot successfully be used to explain Haitian migration. He argues that "academic
models of migration have conceived migration flows as
the consequence of aggregate individual decisions in
response to regional economic inequalities or
disequilibria" (p. 337). He states that U.S.
policymakers have tended to depict individual Haitian
migrants as responding to either political or economic
motivation. But, he then argues, "both the equilibrium model of migration based on individual decisions and the distinction between political and
economic factors impoverish our interpretation of
Haitian migration". Stepick proposes that studies of
Haitian migration should adopt a broader perspective,
and "redirect attention away from the differences between economic and political factors to the integral
linkages between them." (p. 347) I agree with Stepick
and argue, in Chapter III, that historical and

ecological perspectives, as well as cultural considerations, add important dimensions to the study of
Haitian migration. For Haitians, migration has become
a culturally accepted way of resolving problems, it is
for them, *demele*.

Fontaine (1976) and Laguerre (1978, 1984) identify
several waves of Haitian migration, such as those that
occurred during the American occupation of Haiti, and
the emigration of Haitian elite that followed the
election of President Francois Duvalier in the early
sixties. They emphasize the underlying social,
political, and economic causes of these migrations.

Laguerre (1978) examines the role of the Haitian
extended family in internal and external migration.
Its members are linked through consanguineous, legal,
and customary affinal, ritual, and fictive ties. The
Haitian extended family functions as a corporate unit:
"it permits the effective use of limited resources in
peasant economics, facilitates linkage across rural-
urban and class divisions, and supports wider
mobility, including migration to the United States"
(p. 408). Richman's study of the effects of migration
on a Haitian village (1984) showed that most able men
had emigrated, and that most households relied on

remittances from relatives working abroad for survival. She states that in rural Haiti, migration is seen as an effective strategy for young men who are trying to achieve economic autonomy; it also represents a way for their parents to further their own economic interests. Stepick (1984) foresees that Haitians will continue to migrate even if the political situation were to stabilize. Haitians, he says, migrate because there are not enough opportunities for them in Haiti. Allman (1985), on the other hand, suggests that only sustained economic development programs will be able to alter the desire of many Haitians in diverse social and economic circumstances to leave their country. My own data support both their arguments.

A great deal has been written on Haitian communities in the United States. Most of these studies, however, focused on earlier migrations. Buchanan (1979a, 1981), Davidson (1962), Elwell (1977), Fontaine (1976), Glick (1969, 1971), Laguerre (1976, 1978, 1981, and 1984), Sutton (1973), and Walsh (1979) describe established immigrants' communities in the

United States, and the relationships between immigrants and the home society, as well as their adaptation in the host country. These works provide a
framework of reference for the present study.

Graves and Graves (1974:17) note that recent
studies of migration view migrants as interactive individuals who seek to overcome problems confronting
them by choosing among perceived available options. I
argue that Haitian immigrants are social actors who
make choices; they are not simply passive individuals
pushed by circumstances. I note in Chapter IV that,
even though rural migrants tend to be more passive
than their urban counterparts, they are nevertheless
actors. In Haitian rural areas, decisions to migrate
are taken by the extended family, while in America the
migrants from this category act on behalf of their kin
groups.[4]

Philpott (1973:474) first described "migrant
ideology" as "the cognitive model which the migrant
holds as to the nature and goals of his migration".
Laguerre (1984:34) developed this concept into
"migration ideology" as "the thought process by which
an individual perceives the possibility of moving from

one place to another in order to achieve stated personal goals." "People" he argues,

> often see the world as divided into cen-
> ters and peripheries. In this perspec-
> tive, internal/external migration is
> nothing less than an attempt to move
> from a position on the periphery to a
> place at the center, where one can basi-
> cally enjoy a better social environment,
> employment, and sometimes political
> security.

I suggest that all Haitians recognize a social
center and a periphery, and that they strive to
reach a less marginal position, or even a place at
the center. In this analysis, center and periphery
are analytic concepts and do not represent native
terms. However, the meaning of these concepts will
be understood by Haitians. The notion of center is
used here as a metaphor to describe the goals
Haitians strive to achieve, and the place in society
that they aspire to occupy. Migration is a strategy
to move away from a peripheral position, a way to
"make it" to the center. The center is not identi-
cal for all Haitians; it is relative to their position in the social hierarchy.

"Making it" to the center means different things
to different Haitians. Depending on their place in
the social structure, center can mean economic

stability, social advancement, or even political
freedom. *Demele* is the ethos (see Bateson 1972 on
ethos) that guides decisions and choices that
Haitians make. *Demele* appears again and again in
Haitians' speech, in their market and business dealings, in their fighting spirit, and in their
resourcefulness. It is shown here that *demele* comes
into all decision-making processes, and takes two
crucial elements into consideration: the goal one is
trying to reach, and the resources one has at
his/her disposal. At each step one has to weigh
gains against losses: whether to chance the uncertainty of urban life in order to provide a better
education for one's children, or whether to abandon
familiar surroundings and family in order to earn a
better living abroad. Several strategies are available to Haitians who wish to move to the center;
migration is one of them.

Haitian immigrants in the United States

This study defines strategies as the plans that Haitians devise and employ to change situations, to create and take advantage of opportunities. During the process of adaptation, migrants may employ more than one type of strategy. Graves and Graves (1974) suggest that in "individualistic" strategies, migrants rely essentially on their own resources or initiatives for a solution. By contrast, in "group-oriented" strategies migrants turn for help to other people, usually kin, fellow villagers, or migrants from their own ethnic group. Following Graves and Graves, Francis (1984) notes that Haitian immigrants in Philadelphia have adopted an individualistic approach to making a life for themselves in America. My data support their arguments and show that Haitian immigrants from urban areas tend to use "individualistic" strategies, while rural immigrants rely for the most part on "group-oriented" strategies. At the same time, I argue with Francis that urban immigrants use group-oriented strategies as well.[5]

Moreover, the study shows that in the process of migration and adaptation, Haitians of rural background rely mainly on "group-oriented" strategies predicated on kinship amity and kinship ties. It also demonstrates that although urban immigrants ap-pear to use "individualistic" strategies, this is not always the case. Urban immigrants draw extensively on resources available in the host community such as resettlement and social agencies, churches, job and educational programs. Urban Haitians infuse relations with these formal organizations with the spirit of "kinship amity" (Fortes 1969) and "diffused and enduring solidarity" (Schneider 1980).[6]

Laguerre (1984) presents an anthropological perspective of socioeconomic adaptation among Haitian immigrants in New York City. He argues from an approach that views "ethnicity as an adaptive strategy by which individuals and groups define themselves and are defined by others in situational relationships within the context of a structure of dependence and inequality". Dominguez (1975), Buchanan (1979, 1981, 1981b), and Fontaine (1976) argue along similar lines. My data support their views and show that Haitians perceive themselves as a *nasyon* (group, people) different from others, and that they use various strategies to underline their ethnic identity and maintain ethnic boundaries.

Several studies examine the role of ethnic identity in the adaptation process. While Sutton (1973) compares the effects of migration on the formation of ethnic identities among several groups of West Indians, Dominguez (1975) and Glick (1969, 1971, 1975) look at the ways Haitians maintain these boundaries. Their observations are relevant in the context of this study. I argue in Chapters IV and V that Haitian immigrants use language and cultural ideas of *demele* to create social boundaries between themselves and Black Americans.

Others note that language is also a vehicle through which Haitians express and maintain traditional social hierarchies. Buchanan (1979) analyzes the conflict over language use (French vs. Haitian Creole) in a Brooklyn Haitian parish. She claims that in that community, several social classes are vying either to maintain or to change the traditional Haitian social hierarchy. The struggle to maintain or to change this order is expressed in the choice of language (French or Creole) to be used in church services.   Other researchers show that similar patterns are found in other communities; Fontaine (1976) in Boston, and Francis (1984) in Philadelphia.   The data in this study support their findings.

Woldemikael (1985) examines the strategies that Haitian immigrants use in order to achieve their goals in a small midwestern city.   He claims that Haitian immigrants avoid confronting their status as black persons in the larger American society.   They avoid associating with Black Americans, whom they perceive as economically and politically powerless. Instead, they turn to white Americans whom they perceive as powerful patrons.   He claims that this is strictly a strategy aimed at maximizing their economic opportunities.   The data in my study support these observations, but also show that, for Haitians, racial ascription and social status have different meanings.   I argue in Chapters V and VI that, for Haitians, black:white oppositions are more social than racial markers.   Black and white do not necessarily mean only skin color or racial features

- they also indicate social structural relationships.

Other researchers have investigated the boat
people migration, Nachman (1984), Nachman and Widmayer (1984), Bogre (1979), Mattera and Watson
(1983), Richman (1984), Francis (1984). They focus
on a variety of issues such as the social organization of the Haitian communities (Francis 1984), the
implications of this migration on public health
programs (Nachman and Widmayer 1984), and Haitian
workers in the migrant labor system (Mattera and
Watson 1983, Richman 1984). Stepick (1982, 1984a,
1984b, 1984c) has documented the influx of boat
people in Florida and the conflicts surrounding
their legal status in the United States. He examines the impact of the boat people migration on
the Haitian community of Little Haiti, Florida.
Stepick (1984b) discusses the effect of detention on
Haitian boat people released from Miami's Krome
Detention Center. He claims that these "Haitians
have experienced prejudice and discrimination from
all sectors of local society -- White Americans,
Black Americans, and Cubans. Socially, they have
reacted by isolating themselves" (p. ii). Most of

the immigrants in this study had also been incar-
cerated in Krome or other federal detention centers.
They relate similar experiences and exhibit similar
reactions. Chapter IV presents a profile of Haitian
boat people, their reasons for leaving Haiti, and
their experiences in America.

Historical Perspectives

This study uses historical sources to shed light
on the anthropological perspective. Historical data
add an important dimension to the understanding of
the processes that contributed to the development of
contemporary cultural ideas and patterns of social
relations. Rainsford (1805), Davis (1928), Malenfant (1924), Genovese (1979), and Saunders (1818)
provide informative accounts of the dynamics that
precipitated the Haitian War of Independence, the
impact that a successful slave revolt has had on the
development of Haitian national identity, and the
background for understanding present Haitian
economy. Leyburn's (1966) and Metraux' (1960) accounts are helpful in tracing the development of
contemporary Haitian social structure. Leyburn

(1966), Nemours (1952), Logan (1968), Rotberg
(1968), and Nicholls (1979, 1985) offer interpretations of more contemporary political, economic, and
social developments in Haiti.

I would like to point out that between the late
1960's and the end of the 70's, there is a marked
shortage of information on Haiti and Haitians in the
literature.   I attribute this to the influence of
political events in Haiti during that period.
However, with the influx of boat people in the
United States and recent political events in Haiti,
there has also been a renewed interest in ethnographic studies of Haiti.   The various implications of the boat people migration have yet to be
fully documented. This book contributes to this
body of literature by examining the adaptation
process of boat people in upstate New York.

HAITIAN CLASS STRUCTURE

One of the claims I make in this book is that in
order to understand the causes of Haitian emigration
and the adaptation process of Haitian immigrants in
this country, it is also necessary to have a clear

picture of the dynamics that govern social interactions in Haiti.

Leyburn (1966, 1st. ed. 1941) compares the social stratification of Haitian society to that of a caste system. He defines two groups separated by differences in education, religion, social status, and ethnic background. On one hand, members of the Haitian "elite", or upper caste, dominate all government and national institutions, are Catholic, speak French, are educated, and live in urban centers. The "yeomanry" or mass, on the other hand, work the land, are poor, uneducated, speak Creole, are black, and practice *vodou*.[7] Comhaire-Sylvain (1959), writing from a Haitian perspective, suggests that the distinction is more ambiguous - that between the two extremes described by Leyburn there are interstitial classes. Enormous gaps separate a very large, poor, uneducated Class IV from the small elite, or Class I. In-between are two other classes - Classes II and III. Class II is also small and includes the provincial aristocracy, as well as government employees and merchants of large urban centers. She claims that Class III, also referred to as "the people's elite", is the most dynamic segment of the population. I show that it mediates between Classes I and II and Class IV. It is composed of artisans, shopkeepers, factory workers, small town officials, and traders. In my description and analysis, I use Comhaire-Sylvain's terms for class distinctions.

An educational reform program started in the 1920's (as a result of the American occupation), gave impetus to the development of Class III. It provided members of Class IV with the opportunity to acquire skills and education as a way out of their traditional position at the bottom of the social ladder. Although *demele* is a cultural principle and a strategy shared by all Haitians, it is most evident in this category (Class III). Members of this class use *demele* to the fullest in their strategies for upward mobility. One of my informants, who falls into Comhaire-Sylvain's Class III, described Haitian class structure in the following terms: "Les incapables, la masse, ou le peuple: incapables de se supporter, paysans. Les capables: capables de se supporter, emploient les incapables. La bourgeoisie: riches, pas besoin de travailler pour

se soutenir, *chita sou dodin*.   L'elite ou les *gro
zotobre*".   (The   incapables,   the   masses,   the
populace: unable to support themselves, peasants.
The capables: able to support themselves, hire incapables.   The bourgeoisie: rich, do not need to
work for a living, sit idle on a rocking chair [they
take it easy].   The bourgeoisie, the elite are the
"big shots").

All these definitions are valid and useful.
Each touches on sensitive aspects of Haitian social
structure, but implicit in all is the notion of
boundaries and oppositions.   Leyburn emphasizes the
gap between rich and poor, the division between urban and rural.   Comhaire-Sylvain's description emphasizes more the hierarchical structure of Haitian
society and, at the same time, the dynamic, non-
static nature of relationships between the classes.
Class III is only a sub-set of Class IV, and Class
II a sub-set of Class I.   By contrast, strict boundaries exist between these two categories and upward
mobility between Classes III and II is very
restricted.   My informant's point of view reflects
this dual opposition, as seen from an empirical
Class III perspective.   It projects the image both

of struggle and of stasis: struggle in that the
emerging middle class is fighting for better living
conditions and social recognition; and stasis in
that the upper and lower classes remain virtually
untouched.

These nuances are less noticeable in the rural
areas where social distinctions are almost non-
existent.   Referring to the differences between urban and rural Haiti, another informant told me (in
Creole): "*en Ayiti gen de nasyon*" (in Haiti there
are really two countries - literally, nations and
tribes.)   Thus, etic and emic perspectives come
together.   The writers' and my own analysis of the
class system represent the formalized versions,
expressed in technical terms, of Haitians' perceptions of Haitian social structure.

Rural Haitians are still tied to the land,
largely uneducated, and function on the margins of
the national system.   Urban poor and Class III have
their origins among this category.   They reflect attributes from both urban and rural categories.
Their strategies for upward mobility are to acquire
social and cultural markers of the upper classes

that will enable them to attain a position closer to the center.

Thus, the Haitian sociocultural universe can be represented in two major categories of opposition, as shown by the following set of oppositions.[8] These categories of opposition are expressed in terms of structural arrangement and in terms of cultural ideas. Taken together, each column of opposition reflects the two *nasyon* described by my informant. In terms of class structure, the left column represents Class IV and the right one Classes I and II. Class III mediates between the two.

Class IV	Classes I and II
rural	urban
periphery	center
peasant, urban poor	elite
powerlessness	power
Creole	French
Vodou	Christianity
extended family	nuclear family
lack of education	education
black	*white/mulatto*
poverty	wealth
moun sòt	*moun eklere*

The opposition of rural:urban is one of the organizing principles that govern social relations among Haitians. In their process of adaptation to new environments, Haitians seek to re-establish rural-urban oppositions and hierarchical structures that are familiar to them. Haitian communities in America seem to organize themselves naturally along the urban-rural, or *moun sòt-moun eklere*, oppositions.

Most of the internal migration in Haiti is directed toward urban areas, a strategy to move from periphery to center. It is an effort by the rural population to break away from the confines of their social position, to move up from one category to another. This strategy involves the acquisition of upper class markers, such as language, education, religious affiliation, and economic stability.

Urban poor migrate when they realize that the gap between lower and upper classes is, to all effects and purposes, insurmountable. For them, the only way up is out; to leave Haiti. Rural migration is a response to economic and demographic conditions in the countryside, and has been a viable strategy for rural populations for a long time.[9]

FIELDWORK

This research project compared Haitian immigrants in two different settings: a rural environment - the migrant farm labor camps of upstate New York; and an urban milieu - Rochester, New York.[10]

About 150 Haitians came each fall to Wyoming County for the potato harvest.[11] The Rochester population consists of approximately 60 people. Fieldwork started in 1980 in Rochester, and in 1983 in the migrant camps. I observed and talked to most of the migrant workers, as well as to most of the Haitian immigrants in the Rochester community. I kept detailed notes and a journal on my participant-observation and talks with the immigrants. I participated in public events, church meetings, trials, clinics, and home visits in both locations. I also conducted formal interviews with 43 informants, 30 in the migrant camps and 13 in Rochester.[12]

Among the 43 informants who were interviewed, thirteen were women (4 in Rochester and 9 in the migrant camps) and 30 were men (9 in Rochester and 21 in the migrant camps). These numbers are fairly representative of the sex-ratio in both locations.

I do not have exact figures on the number of small children in Rochester and in the migrant camps. I can only say that in 1983 (first migrant season), there were substantially more family units and children under 6 than during the 1984 season. In Rochester, there were fewer family units with children. In both locations I only met one child over the age of 6.

All the immigrants interviewed were of rural or low income urban backgrounds. All but two were boat people. The migrant farm workers lived in immigrant communities in Florida, from which they were recruited into the migrant stream. The Rochester group consisted of former migrant farm workers and others who came to the city to join relatives and friends. All the immigrants spoke Haitian Creole; few could speak French. Their level of education varied. Most had only a few years of formal education, and some could neither read nor write.

During the period when the research was carried out, the immigrants' legal status was still uncertain.[13] The INS (Immigration and Naturalization Service) maintained that they had left Haiti for economic reasons, and could not be considered as political refugees. The Haitians claimed that in Haiti, politics and economy were so intertwined that the difference was hard for them to perceive. Boat people were granted I-94 visas which allowed them the right to remain and work in this country, pending a resolution of their immigration status. I-94 holders can be subjected to exclusion or deportation hearings at any time. The uncertainty of their legal status has been a source of stress for boat people, and has influenced their strategies of adaptation.

However, with the Immigration Reform and Control Act of 1986, there is some hope that those who had entered the U.S. before Jan. 1, 1982, will be able to adjust their visa status to that of permanent resident.

The nature of seasonal farm work, and the work and living conditions in migrant farm labor camps, made it nearly impossible to arrange to meet people ahead of time. I interviewed whoever was there and had time to talk, alone or in a group. Thus, informants were chosen at random, and sampling techniques were not used.

The migrant population is very mobile. Workers come and go during the season, change camps, etc. Occasionally entire camps leave overnight. The Rochester population is also very unstable. People change addresses often and it is difficult to keep track of them. Although all the immigrants were willing to talk to me, some were reluctant to have their conversations recorded on tape, fearing possible political or legal reprisals.

Several methods of data collection were used. Life histories were gathered: structured interviews, informal conversations, and elicitation sessions were conducted in Haitian Creole. Whenever possible, tape recordings of these speech events were made with the informant's permission. Field notes were always taken to record specific information and contextual details and observations. The information thus gathered covers a variety of topics.

Participant-observation was an important component of the data gathering process: it provided information on group dynamics, social relations, and language use. Interviews with community and religious leaders, political figures, service providers, and employers yielded information on the

support systems that Haitians use, the social networks they build, their legal problems, and the
dynamics of the Haitian community, as well as data
on how Haitians are perceived in their host communities.

THE SETTINGS

Migrant Camps

The potato fields of Wyoming County in the
Genesee valley stretch for miles. The migrant
workers' camps are sometimes built on the edges of
fields, lost in the countryside. The casual passer-
by would not even notice the low, shabby buildings.
Potato pickers are the lowest paid seasonal farm
helpers, and work in this crop has traditionally
been among the lowest status of all types of migrant
farm work (Mattera and Watson 1983:10). Potato harvesting is mainly stoop labor and conditions in the
fields are often unsanitary. Growers are still not
required to provide drinking water and hygienic
facilities in the fields for the workers, some of
them pregnant women, who work up to 12 hours a day.
The pay is also very poor. A picker gets a quarter

per bag of potatoes - each bag weighs 75 lbs. On a good day, a good worker can fill 100 bags, and some exceptional pickers working in pairs have filled up to 350 bags.

Fieldwork was conducted in Wyoming County during the 1983 and 1984 Fall harvesting seasons. "Camps are in" by the first week of September and work goes on until the end of October. Through the BOCES Geneseo Migrant Center, I located and visited seven camps housing potato pickers. In the Fall of 1983, I concentrated on one Haitian camp. The following year, I interviewed Haitian workers in two Haitian camps and one mixed camp. By "Haitian camp" I mean camps in which the majority of the workers are of Haitian origin. A "mixed camp" is one in which workers come from a variety of ethnic groups.

I collected a total of thirty life histories in the migrant farm labor camps during the 1983 and 1984 migrant seasons; nine from women and twenty-one from men. Both years I visited the camps on a regular basis, in the evenings after the workers had come back from the fields, and during the day when I had a chance to talk more freely to anyone who had stayed home. During these two seasons, I had the

opportunity to observe the migrant workers in a
variety of settings. I saw them at home, at work,
and outside of their migrant environment. I accompanied some workers to dental clinics, saw them at
ESL (English as a Second Language) classes. I also
took part in special programs offered by the BOCES
Geneseo Migrant Center. Each year the Center or-
ganizes several cultural events for the workers and
an "All Camps Day" during which entertainment, arts
and craft instruction, and games are provided
together with refreshments and dinner. These events
take place at the Center and offer a great opportunity to observe the social interaction between
migrant workers, social service providers, and members of the community, as well as among migrant
workers of different ethnic backgrounds. I also observed the behavior of Haitian migrant workers outside of the camp environment, and the rate of active
participation in the various activities offered.
The Center also offers several in-camp programs:
health and educational programs, and recreational
and cultural events, during which artists, poets,
musicians, and craftsmen are invited to conduct
workshops in the camps. It also features a Folk

Arts Program, funded by the New York State Council for the Arts, which is aimed at collecting, preserving, and disseminating traditional folk arts forms. At the end of the season, a display of the migrants' artwork is organized. The 1984 exhibit was held at the Museum of Afro-American and African Art in Buffalo.

I visited mixed as well as Haitian camps in order to find out more about race relations in the migrant stream and the social organization in each milieu. Although all the interviews the first year were conducted in an all-Haitian camp, I also visited and participated in programs in other camps. It takes time for the observer to become accustomed to the harsh environment and physical conditions of migrant camps. In addition, sometimes clearances have to be obtained from the grower before one is allowed to visit the workers.

Life in the camps is grim. Each family occupies a room; single men are grouped in "bull pens". A common kitchen, dining/recreation room, and communal showers complete the setting. Each camp has its particular atmosphere. Some growers try to provide accommodations that are a step above the minimum required by State regulations - others barely pass inspection. After work, the dust coated workers, who come home exhausted, shower and prepare dinner. During the evenings and on weekends, workers can participate in ESL (English as a Second Language) and other programs run by the Migrant Center, health and dental clinics, as well as recreational ac- tivities. Gambling is a favorite pastime in the camps. Black American workers play a variety of card games, while Haitians usually play dominoes. Music is an important element of camp life. Haitian migrants play the guitar, drums and a variety of percussion instruments. Cassette players are indis- pensable. They serve as a link between the im- migrant and home communities, and tapes containing messages and music are constantly being played.

The Eastern migrant stream is composed of several ethnic groups: Black Americans, Hispanics, West Indians, Native Americans and some White Americans. Potato pickers, as part of this stream, are predominantly Black Americans and West Indians (mainly Haitians). Some camps are ethnically mixed, while others have a homogeneous population. Haitians began to appear in the Eastern stream in

1980. Over the past two years their number has increased substantially. In 1983 and 1984, they ac-
counted for about half of the potato harvesters.
The presence of Haitians has created new problems
for farmers, crew leaders, and support service
providers. These people were not ready to deal
with Haitians; they did not understand their language, their culture, nor their work habits.

Haitian workers have been grossly exploited.
They were sometimes assigned to pick poor tracks,
given lower grade accommodations, and assessed extra
fees by Crew Leaders. Recently, Haitians have been
more aware of their legal rights and are starting to
form their own crews.

An American farmer described Haitian migrants as
"conscientious, good workers eager to learn and
earn". He added, however, that they had trouble understanding the "whole picture". For example, instead of picking the potatoes in a straight line
after the digger had gone through and before the
truck came along to pick the filled bags, they would
scatter eagerly all over the fields. The Haitians
find farm labor a good source of income, even though
the conditions are harsh. Most say that they have

too many responsibilities at home to overlook any opportunity to earn some money.

Some enterprising individuals have left the migrant stream to settle in cities and towns where, they believe, better opportunities exist. Many of them elected to stay in Rochester. A comparison of the number of former migrants who have settled in Rochester between 1982 and 1984 shows that fewer people elected to leave the stream in 1983 and 1984, as compared to 1982. As time goes by, the immigrant population is organizing itself into communities, and new networks are being established, making it harder for an individual to abandon what has become a familiar environment, and to face the unknown once more.

ROCHESTER, NEW YORK

The first boat people arrived in Rochester in the summer of 1980. They had been abandoned downtown by a crew leader whose promises of work never materialized. It was a tragic situation. The immigrants could not speak English and the city did not have any Creole interpreters. A few

Haitians and some area churches helped those who elected to remain in the city get settled, and the others return to Florida. This core population is well-established now and has attracted relatives and friends to the city. Another group of Haitian immigrants chose to come to Rochester after the Ray Brook Detention Center in the Adirondacks was ordered to close in 1982. The landmark Spellman decision, handed down by the U.S. District Court for the Southern District of Florida, ordered the release of all Haitian entrants held in federal detention centers.

The Rochester immigrants tend to form small groups according to their area of origin in Haiti, or according to their time of arrival in the city. They live in the predominantly black neighborhoods of Bay Street, North Clinton and Parsell Avenues. Members of each group maintain strong ties and usually share housing and resources. However, there is not much contact between the groups. Area churches and social service agencies sponsor a variety of assistance programs and resettlement services for the immigrants, such as counseling, job training, health, and educational programs. Law firms offer pro bono legal assistance to individuals who are called for deportation and exclusion hearings by the INS (Immigration and Naturalization Services).

I have been involved with the Haitian community in Rochester since 1980, when the first group of boat people arrived in the city. I knew, visited, and talked with close to forty of the estimated sixty Haitian boat people who lived in Rochester between June 1983 and March 1984. During that time, I conducted thirteen formal interviews, four with women and seven with men. The lack of cohesion in the community, and the demands of work and urban life precluded any form of rigorous sampling. The immigrants changed addresses often, roommates would quarrel and move in with somebody else, many left town, telephone numbers and work schedules would change. As in the case of the migrant population, the formal interviews consist of a self-selected population.

I was interested in comparing adaptive strategies of Haitian immigrants in two settings: in the migrant labor system and in an urban environment. I also wanted to explore the ways in which resettlement took place in Rochester. For example, how did immigrants find housing and jobs; what were the dynamics of resettlement - how did the immigrants get along in the community, what cultural and social factors influenced the adaptation process; and how much the Haitians' experiences as migrant workers affected their choice of strategies.

The distinct atmosphere of the two settings - the rural and the urban - called for different fieldwork techniques. The length of the migrant season and the need to gather as much information as possible in such a short time lent a feeling of urgency and intensity to fieldwork in the migrant camps. In this unusual environment, relationships developed rapidly. Individuals were more willing to confide, to talk about themselve. We were all aware that after the eight to ten weeks that the season lasted, we probably would never meet again. It was an emotionally and physically draining experience. Fieldwork in the city was very different. The pace was slower. The urgency was replaced by the intimacy and familiarity of long-term relationships. I also had to take into account the striking difference in organization of the two settings. The migrant workers lived together in camps, whereas the urban group was scattered in the city and involved in a variety of occupations. Over the years, I have formed lasting friendships and gained a fair knowledge of the community. Ours is an ongoing relationship. It would be unfair to ignore that I am still involved with the community and that this long-term involvement has given me a better understanding of the adaptation process.

Following an initial meeting during which I explained the purpose of my fieldwork, I started meeting the immigrants individually and in small groups. I was able to use a meeting room in a local church that was accessible to most of the population. I often visited the immigrants in their homes, took them on errands, accompanied them to court, and was invited to social functions. We communicated often by telephone. They knew that they could always get in touch with me, and still do, to discuss personal problems or to keep me posted on events in the community. This way of communicating allowed the informants the freedom to initiate conversations and to concentrate on matters important to them.

Besides talking to the Haitian immigrants themselves, I also got in touch with ministers, lawyers, employers, and agencies involved with the Haitian population. I met with the Congressman responsible for the district in which most Haitian immigrants lived to find out his views on immigration issues.

Several structural and cultural issues emerged from the outset of my involvement with the Rochester community. The first concerned the lack of community spirit and cohesion among the immigrants. There are several small, but separate groups of immigrants in the city. Although the immigrants in each group knew of the other Haitians in Rochester, there was a definite lack of interest in getting to know people from other groups. I also noticed that the urban population faced many more demands as compared to the migrant population. The immigrants constantly talked about the demands of urban life, the cost of living, and strategies for "making it". They complained of illnesses and related dreams that reflected a definite connection to social and psychological stress. Another issue was the greater influence of external cultural factors on this population. Contrary to the migrant workers, who lived in a more homogeneous environment (small agricultural communities and farm labor camps), the urban population is embedded in the larger context of an American city. Its networks include a variety of individuals from different ethnic, social, cultural, and class backgrounds. Compared with the migrant population, I found the urban immigrants to be more aware of cultural differences and ethnic diversity, and constantly assessing their cultural heritage in light of other cultures. Among them there was a more acute, keen sense of their own ethnic identity and national pride, while at the same time a strong desire to be integrated in the larger context of American society.

According to a local clergyman who has been involved with the Haitian community since 1980, the level of employment among the immigrants is high and employers find Haitians good workers. However, he was surprised that they are reluctant to organize community-based activities, associations and emergency trust funds. He argues that their lack of trust in others and reluctance to volunteer help and services are survival mechanisms and a result of their experiences at home. The former Haitian government forbade the organization of interest groups and political gatherings. It enforced these prohibitions ruthlessly. There is some validity in this interpretation, but I propose that the reasons behind the Haitians' distrust have their roots in Haiti's history and its hierarchical social structure. The rural and urban poor populations have always been isolated and kept from participating in economic and political decisions. They have always been marginal people who have had to make it on their own, with no help from others. *Demele*, in this case, carries a stronger meaning: to make it on one's own, in spite of difficulties. This also explains the reluctance of Haitians to accept welfare, a decision that community service providers have attributed to the immigrants' "Calvinistic" work ethic. The concept of *demele* also motivates the immigrants to enroll in ESL classes, avoid what they consider wasteful expenses (such as alcohol and drugs), and stay out of trouble.

Stepick (1984) observes that Haitian immigrants (he refers here only to boat people) do not conform to the common negative stereotype of unskilled, unsuccessful individuals looking for an easy way to make money. Instead, they are highly motivated, hardworking, and anxious to become part of American society. As this study shows, the immigrants had already tried several avenues in Haiti and were able, even in the face of adversity, to accomplish some of their goals. According to informants, *moun eklere*, those who possess enough skills and other resources, such as education and knowledge of English, are able to integrate successfully. The others, or *moun sòt*, unskilled, uneducated rural people, remain isolated in farm worker communities.

Contrary to what informants may think, there are individuals in both groups who say that they are "making it". They are those who are good at what they do, who have been able to apply their former skills here - as farm workers, tailors or welders - and feel happy with what they are doing, as well as where they are in relation to their goals.

The data also show that emigration and migration are sometimes ways to create not only a geographi- cal, but also a social distance from home. Those who chose internal migration or temporary emigration keep ties alive with their home communities. Those who could not go back because of political, legal or other circumstances, and those who elected not to go back, have to make different kinds of choices: their center - social, economic or geographical - is no longer a bounded Haitian center. There is no fixed center for all Haitian immigrants; each one defines his or her center differently. It is determined by where one wants to be and the goals one wants to achieve.

*   *   *

My particular situation, as a Haitian anthropologist studying Haitians, highlights some general issues regarding the nature of fieldwork, as well as Haitian ideas about social relations and class distinctions. The interaction between anthropologist and informant revealed a great deal about how Haitians organize and describe their social universe, how their cultural ideas regarding social hierarchy in Haiti guide their interactions in America, and where I was to fit in their world. Each time I met a new individual or group of immigrants in Rochester or in the camps, I was submitted to intense questioning in order to establish my Haitian identity and "credentials", and map the course for social interaction. An interesting

process took place during which my social and
regional backgrounds, my knowledge of Haitian Creole
and customs, and of certain cultural and historical
facts were assessed. The questioning followed a
similar pattern: "so, you speak Creole!", "where did
you learn to speak Creole?". When I would answer
"*se Ayisyen m'ye*" (I am Haitian), they would look me
over and comment on my appearance. For example,
people of rural origins would say: "I've never seen
a Haitian like you" or "where I come from there are
no Haitians like you". Others would simply con-
clude, "then you must be from Port-au-Prince".
Questions about my family would follow. "What's
your father's name?" "What did he do?" "Why did he
leave Haiti?" "When?" The conversation would then
touch on more personal information. "Are you
married?" "Do you have children?" Or, "what was
wrong with you - how come you did not have a child
before you left home, if you were already 18?" When
they were satisfied that I really belonged, a joke
about my complexion usually followed, such as: "*ou
se Ayisyen po lanvè*" (you are just a Haitian with
her skin inside-out!) or a wise statement like
"light skin or dark skin, it does not matter, we are

all Haitians". After I had passed this initial
test, we would reminisce about home, what we missed
most, the fruits, foods, the ocean, climate, the
music etc., and then go on talking about more personal and immediate concerns.

Sometimes we would also negotiate on the form of
address to be used. I did not particularly like the
formal form "Madame", especially since according to
Haitian etiquette, I would be "madame Alec".[14] Con-
sequently, I suggested that my first name be used.
One informant told me that it was impossible for him
to address me in such an informal way, that "at home
it was not done like that". When I suggested that
we were in America, he thought it over and chose instead to call me "Sè Rose" (sister Rose).

Although I was accepted as a fellow Haitian,
there were still questions about the reasons for my
presence in the camps. My association with the
BOCES Geneseo Migrant Center - as a Consultant for
the preparation of the <u>Haitian Component</u> of the
<u>Migrant Heritage Studies Kit</u> - gave me an official
status. The workers perceived me as a *patron*, one
who knew the American way and could help them understand it. In their perception of hierarchy, I was

closer to the center and could pull them away from periphery. They also saw me as a problem solver and felt free to discuss matters of concern to them. These perspectives allowed me to develop a broader vision of who they were, how and why they came here, as well as an insight into their broad range of experiences. My identity and involvement with the Rochester community was easier to explain. Since I knew both worlds (the Haitian and the American), I could act as a cultural broker. I lived in the city, had a family, acted as interpreter and expert witness at INS hearings, and performed a variety of small favors, such as helping with job application forms, translating letters, giving directions, etc. Community service providers, employers, religious and community leaders accepted me as an anthropologist and an advocate for the Haitian community.

The following chapters describe and analyze the adaptation process of Haitian immigrants of rural and urban poor origins who have entered the United States between 1978 and 1982. Chapter II presents an overview of Haiti's history and ecology. It demonstrates that Haiti's contemporary social structure, and its economic and political institutions

ture, and its economic and political institutions are linked to these factors. Chapter III gives an overview of Haitian migration.

Chapter IV examines the roots of Haitian emigration. It analyzes emigration as an outcome of internal "push" away from poverty, demographic pressures, lack of opportunity, and hierarchical social structure, as well as external "pulls" of perceived opportunities elsewhere. It focuses on the latest wave of migration of Haitians from rural and low income urban origins in the United States. It suggests that migration is one of the adaptive strategies that Haitians use, a form of *demele*. It is a culturally accepted way for Haitians of rural and poor urban origins to move from a position at the periphery to one closer to the center. It also offers a description and analysis of the migration process.

Chapter V concentrates on the adaptation process of Haitian immigrants in the migrant labor system. The migrant stream is a special type of American milieu. It is a rural environment with a distinctive character and established structure. Haitian immigrants who enter this system bring with them

resolving conflicts. In this environment, the two systems are engaged in an interplay during which both are transformed. It suggests that cultural ideas embodied in the concept of *demele* and a strong desire to "make it" help the immigrants in their adaptation to migrant labor.

Chapter VI presents Haitian boat people in an urban context - Rochester, New York. It analyzes the ways in which Haitian cultural ideas regarding hierarchy, class distinctions, and the opposition of rural and urban categories influence the immigrants' strategies of adaptation. This Chapter demonstrates that the same cultural factors that informed the decisions of Haitians to leave their country and to join the migrant stream also influence their decision to come to Rochester. However, it points out that those immigrants who move to an urban environment have different characteristics. They have a history of prior internal migration in Haiti, have lived in an urban center, and have some education and skills. Their center is no longer a Haitian center. The focal point is shifting toward America, as they take advantage of opportunities offered there.

Chapter VII presents some conclusions drawn from the previous chapters, and considers the contribution that this study makes towards a better understanding of problems related to migration, immigration, and adaptation.

CHAPTER II

HISTORICAL AND CONTEMPORARY PERSPECTIVES

This chapter emphasizes the importance of historical and ecological perspectives for the understanding
of contemporary social processes. Both have contributed to a large extent to the formation of Haitian
"conscience collective" (Durkheim 1933), from which
individuals draw to guide them in their choices of
strategies. The concepts used in this analysis:
demele, hierarchy, opposition of social categories
such as urban-rural, as well as strategies and adaptation, can best be understood in light of Haiti's history and ecology.

HAITI

The island of Hispaniola is shared by the
Dominican Republic, which occupies its eastern side,
and the Republic of Haiti (about 10,700 sq. mi,
roughly one-third of the total surface). Discovered
in 1492 by Christopher Columbus, Hispaniola is the
second largest of the Caribbean islands. It lies

about 400 miles south of Nassau and 50 miles south-
west of Cuba. It is bordered by the Atlantic Ocean
to the North and the Caribbean Sea to the South. Its
central location in the Caribbean Basin made it a
valuable asset in colonial times;

> Its topographical position is such as to
> command the entrance to the Gulf of
> Mexico from the Southwest and to give it
> importance on the great ocean highway
> leading from Europe and the United
> States to the isthmus which joins the
> two Americas and which must, in the
> opinion of many, open someday a con-
> venient passage between the great oceans
> (Bureau of the American Republics,
> 1893).

Haiti is very mountainous. Its original Arawak
name, *Ayti*, means "land of mountains". Logan (1968:
6) notes that, relative to area, Haiti is even more
mountainous than Switzerland. The variety of
climates, vegetation, and terrains found in this area
(the size of Maryland) is rather surprising, from
coastal plains to extensive mountain ranges, valleys,
forests and savannahs. Its coastline is very detailed
and dotted by a number of smaller islands. Two large
peninsulae stretching westward give Haiti the peculiar
profile of "a crocodile that is about to swallow the
desiccated satellite island of La Gonave and, in time,

attack the neighboring nations of Cuba and Jamaica" (Rotberg, 1971:5).

Temperatures and rainfall vary widely between the coastal areas and the mountains. Average temperatures range between 72 degrees Fahrenheit in the winter months and 83 degrees in the summer. While in the mountains it can be rather cold (as low as 50 degrees), it hardly gets warmer than 95 degrees in the lowlands. Sea breezes that cool down the coastal areas also increase evaporation and contribute to the aridity in some areas where rainfall is already low. Trade winds, blowing mainly from the northeast in the winter and from the southeast in the summer, control the rainy seasons. They bring large amounts of rainfall to higher elevations, while the lowlands often suffer from droughts. Although several short streams water the plains, their output is very inconsistent. They swell with the rains, but quickly dry out.

Because of the unusual topography of the country, only a small percentage of the land can be cultivated. Deforestation and subsequent erosion are major problems. Trees have been cut down to be converted into charcoal, the only source of fuel. Slash and burn techniques are still used to clear and prepare land for planting. The lack of adequate irrigation systems in the plains further reduces the area of arable land that can be efficiently cultivated. In 1978, out of a total of 545 thousand hectares of arable land, 340 thousand hectares were permanently under cultivation and only 70 thousand were properly irrigated (United Nations ECLA, 1981). It is difficult to farm the slopes with the available techniques. Rain water rushing down the steep mountain slopes carries down valuable top soil, carving deep gullies. Irrigation is a must in most of the plains and valleys, and the Northern Plain is the only area that can be successfully exploited without additional irrigation. The Artibonite Valley, which formerly was Haiti's bread basket, and the Plain of the Cul-de-sac are no longer very productive. The irrigation systems (built by the French) were destroyed during the 1791 revolution and have never been restored (Rotberg 1971: 13).

As landholdings are small, farming methods still primitive, and fertilizers scarcely used, it is not surprising that the agricultural yield is small. Farming is still done at the subsistence level, although some cash crops are also grown. There are few large farms where agriculture is done on a commercial scale (Leyburn 1966).

The diversity of landscapes is mirrored by the variety of agricultural products grown on the island. While coffee flourishes in the mountains and some pine forests still remain, savannah grasslands cover the central plain. The main crops are rice, bananas, coffee, sugar cane, maize, beans, potatoes, cacao. Bananas, coffee, sisal and sugar cane are the most lucrative cash crops.

Although Haiti's coastline is very extensive, fishing is not an important industry. There are no canning factories, nor exportation of seafood products. Fish is a staple of the population who inhabit the coastal areas; little of it is sold fresh in markets in the interior. Large amounts of salt and dried fish are imported (United Nations ECLA, 1981).

Haiti's economy is mainly dependent on agriculture. In 1970, 74.9% of the economically active population was employed in the agricultural sector, 7.2% in manufacturing, and 1.5% in basic services (United Nations ECLA, 1981). Although sugar cane and coffee processing plants have been in operation since colonial times, some light industries like sisal and tourism have traditionally contributed to the economy. Bauxite has been mined with increasing success (640 thousand tons in 1979, up from 346 in 1960), but there are neither petroleum related industries nor heavy manufacturing in Haiti (United Nations ECLA, 1981). Recently, foreign companies, attracted by the availability of cheap labor, have established fac- tories in Haiti. A Haitian worker earns on the average $3.20 per day and receives few fringe benefits, while the government offers attractive tax packages to investing companies and imposes few labor restrictions. In recent years, several industries for the manufacture of electronic components, garments, baseballs, and automotive parts have opened around the capital, Port-au-Prince. However, according to Jean- Claude Duvalier the government was actively pursuing a program of industrialization and decentralization in order to attract new businesses to other parts of the country.

In 1969, the population of Haiti was estimated at 4,768,101 inhabitants by the Institut Haitien de Statistique (Rotberg, 1971: 262). Since then it is estimated that this number has grown by 2.4% annually during the period 1975-1980, from an average of 2.1%

between 1960 and 1965. While the birth rate has decreased from 44.5/thousand inhabitants for the period 1960-1965, to 41.8 for 1975-1980, life expectancy has also increased from 47.9 years (1960-1965) to 57.1 (1975--1980). In 1970, 10.4% of the population lived in Port-au-Prince compared to 6.6% in 1960 (United Nations ECLA, 1981), and 50% of the rural population occupies about 17% of available land (Marshall 1979:3).

Haiti is a country of contrasts. Its diversity of landscapes reflects its social diversity, its hierarchy and oppositions: great wealth and great poverty, power and subordination, urban and rural cultures, elite and peasants, Christianity and *vodou*, French and Creole, extended families and nuclear units, great beginnings and present poverty and strife.

HISTORICAL BACKGROUND

In 1805, Marcus Rainsford, "Captain of the Third West-India Regiment" and English observer of the War of Independence, wrote of the new country that was *Hayti*:

> Should they adhere to the basis on which
> they have founded their proceedings, and
> remain unmolested by European powers,
> they may arrive at the most enviable
> state of grandeur and felicity; but
> should any evil spirits obtain a footing
> amongst them, and interrupt the harmony
> which may otherwise be maintained, by
> occasioning factions to arise from old
> contentions, or new divisions, they will
> in all probability fulfill the predict-
> ion of Edwards, by becoming "savages in
> the midst of society, without peace,
> security, agriculture, or property"
> (1805: 360).

Amid such predictions, Haiti took its place among the free nations of the world, the first colony where Negro slaves repudiated their masters and the second free nation in the Americas.

Haiti's present economic situation, social problems, history of political oppression, and cultural diversity can best be understood in light of its past history.

In 1492, when Columbus first went to the New World, Spain was completing the re-conquest of its territories from the Moors (Logan 1968:27). Hispaniola became the first permanent Spanish settlement in the Americas, and represented the hopes of the Spanish monarchy for economic and political dominance in Europe.

Hispaniola - then called *Ayti* or *Quisqueya* - was
inhabited by Tainos, an Arawak-speaking Indian tribe.
Hard labor imposed by the conquerors and the introduction of new diseases quickly took their toll.   In
1508, only 60,000 Indians were left from the million
who inhabited the island at the time of the conquest.
By 1548, the Spanish historian Oviedo noted that only
500 Indians remained (Logan 1968:11).   To alleviate
the misery of those whom the settlers referred to as
"dirty dogs" and whom the romantics called "noble
savages", Las Casas (a Dominican priest and advocate
of the Indian cause), proposed to

> substitute, in the place of those he
> wished to liberate from slavery in their
> own country, the inhabitants of a dis-
> tant one, whom he appeared to consider
> more capable of labor, and more patient
> under sorrow (Rainsford 1805:30).

Thus, in 1517, the mass importation of Negro slaves
into the New World began. By 1560, less than a century after the Spanish conquest, the island was significantly changed. A few Indians remained, but
30,000 African slaves farmed the land and worked the
gold mines for 2,000 Spaniards.

Spain's *siglo de oro* came to an end in 1588, with
the defeat of its Armada, and the years that followed
saw it busy at war in Europe. The colonies were

floundering: revenues fell, English, French, and Dutch buccaneers raided Hispaniola freely, and Sir Francis Drake pillaged the colony's capital Santo Domingo. In 1697, under the treaty of Ryswick, Spain ceded the western third of Hispaniola to France. A new era began.

During the next one hundred years, the new colony, Saint Domingue, prospered. It became known as "the Pearl of the Antilles". More slaves were brought in to tend the plantations. Coffee, indigo, sugarcane, and cotton were farmed with great success. Roads, irrigation systems, and new cities were built, and ports opened to accommodate the heavy traffic, while plantation owners accumulated great wealth. In 1783, the colony produced two-thirds of all French-grown tropical produce and as much sugar as all the British possessions in the Caribbeans (Rotberg 1971:31). On the eve of the French Revolution, Saint Domingue was responsible for more than 40% of the foreign trade of France (idem:32).

The period of French rule coincided with the Age of Enlightenment in Europe and the colony participated in the intellectual life of the mother country (Logan 1968). The population followed closely the political

debates, which eventually led to the French Revolution. These ideas in turn influenced the liberation
movement in the colony.

But Saint Domingue was not without its problems.
In 1791, there were 36,000 whites, 28,000 *gens de
couleur*, and about half a million slaves (Leyburn
1966:16). The relationship between the social groups
was, at best, tense. The Whites, also called *creoles*,
consisted of two groups, the *grand blancs* and the
petits blancs. The *grand blancs* were the rich plantation owners, merchants and colonial administrators.
Shopkeepers, overseers, artisans and some who owned
small farms were the *petits blancs*. The *gens de
couleur*, also called *affranchis*, or free people of
color, included all individuals of African heritage,
those slaves who had been freed, and children of
whites and slaves. This group played an important
role in Haiti's history. It was instrumental first in
shaping the slave liberation and, later, the independence movements in the colony. Many sons of wealthy
planters had been educated in France where they became
acquainted with the revolutionary ideals of liberty
and equality. The slaves who came from several
regions of West Africa worked the plantations. Their

housing and working conditions were dismal, and corporal punishment was often used.

Leyburn (1966:16) traces the present class system of Haiti to the frictions that existed between the *gens de couleur* and the *petits blancs* in colonial times. Undoubtedly, these social problems were among the reasons precipitating the Haitian Revolution. *Petits blancs* resented the wealth, education, and social standing of the *affranchis*, specially the fact that they, as whites, were excluded from high society, while sons of former slaves were admitted. These tensions led to the passage of discriminatory laws against all people of color. The *Code Noir*, promulgated in 1685, during the reign of Louis XIV, which guaranteed full civil rights to all people of color and freed slaves, was progressively abrogated by colonial authorities. Thus began a period of strife and recriminations that culminated in 1791, with the first black revolt. "The *grands blancs* wanted equality with the metropolitan Frenchmen; middle-class French colonials wanted equality with *grands blancs*; *petits blancs* believed in equality for all whites. Upper-class colored colonials interpreted Liberty, Equality, and Fraternity exclusively with reference to

themselves. The Negro slaves had to win their freedom
by force of arms" (Logan 1968:89).

The first revolt took place on August 14, 1791.
It was a bloody uprising. Plantations burned, blacks
and whites were slaughtered, and slaves fled the plantations. Several interpretations have been advanced
about the reasons precipitating the revolt of 1791.
Genovese (1979), Rainsford (1805), and Lundahl (1979)
allude to the injustices of a system that used the
labor of thousands to the benefit of a few and could
only engender resentment and anger. Nemours (1956)
sees in the 1791 revolt the culmination of a series of
slave uprisings that had started shortly after the
beginning of the slave trade. He argues that the
Blacks and free people of color who had participated
in the American War of Independence in 1779 had observed the tactics, methods, and political organization of the American revolutionaries, saw that they
had succeeded, and applied them to the resolution of
their own problems at home. They learned from that
experience "..*que c'etait seulement dans
l'Independance qu'ils pouvaient jouir de tous leurs
droits, en toute assurance..*" [..that they could be

sure to enjoy all their rights, only if they were independent.. (Nemours 1956:VIII)]. The ideals of the
French Revolution of 1789 also had their impact on
those free people of color who had been educated in
France. They understood the value of St. Domingue to
France and resented the injustices of the colonial
system. The slaves who had observed the struggles between the free people of color and the whites over the
restitution of the rights accorded to all people of
color in the Code Noir, gradually came to realize the
strength that their number afforded them and joined in
the revolt (Rotberg 1971:42).

One of the main factors that made the War of Independence possible was the cohesiveness of the slave
population. Metraux (1937:61) notes that the tradition of *marronage*[15] was important not only in the
development of the revolution, but also in safeguard-
ing African traditions. It is mainly through the
practice of *vodou* that the slaves achieved the
cohesiveness that allowed them to mobilize effectively
for insurrection. From the ethnic diversity that
characterized the slave population, a new pattern of
behavior was created (*vodou*) in response to new circumstances (expatriation and slavery). It is also

vodou that has kept the peasantry unified, and may have contributed to the isolation of the modern day Haitian rural population. The leaders of the slave revolt made judicious use of *vodou* beliefs and rituals to crystallize the population and spur it into action. The fighting and devastation that ensued were so intense that in 1793, the Colonial government had to proclaim the emancipation of all slaves in St. Domingue, and in February 1794, the National Legislative Assembly in Paris abolished slavery in all French colonies (Leyburn 1941; Lundahl 1975; Davis 1967; Genovese 1979; Rainsford 1805).

Between 1791 and 1804 several leaders emerged: Toussaint, Rigaud, Dessalines, and Christophe. Toussaint, an ex-slave, had the support of the black population, while Rigaud, a well-to-do *mulatto*, (another term for *gens de couleur*), was backed by the *affranchis*. These two groups alternately formed and broke alliances. This pattern survived into present day oppositions and underlies the traditional social cleavages that shaped Haiti's history and its present class divisions. Toussaint, an astute politician and skilled soldier, often referred to as the "artisan of Haiti's independence", died captive in France in

April, 1803. In November of the same year, Napoleon's army surrendered to the revolutionary forces and on January 1, 1804, Independence was proclaimed.

Thus, tattered and impoverished, Haiti began under Dessalines what was to become a long and arduous journey toward nationhood. Plantations had been burned, irrigation systems, cities and ports destroyed. The struggle between whites and blacks became a struggle between *mulattos* and blacks. Since only the *mulattos* and a small number of former slaves had received formal education, government and power remained in the hands of a few. This pattern still persists. Blacks were given land under a progressive land reform plan designed by Toussaint and later enforced by Dessalines and Petion. In the end, this attempt to redistribute resources evenly among all citizens became one of the major sources of Haiti's economic problems and maintained what Leyburn refers to as the two-caste system. The rural population remained attached to the land and to farming. The plots acquired after independence have been subdivided and overfarmed and today can hardly produce enough to feed the peasants. It also became very difficult to maintain large plantations on which sugar, indigo, and coffee could be grown and processed at an industrial level. Cultivation at the plantation level was the main source of colonial revenues (Leyburn 1941; Davis 1928; Nicholls 1979; Beard 1853).

Dessalines briefly led the country after independence. He was assassinated in October 1804, after a short reign of terror. The Republic was then split into two independent states. The South and West was led by Petion (a *mulatto*), and the North was led by Christophe (a former slave). Both tried to build a solid economic and political infrastructure. Petion, a benevolent man, established a republic; Christophe, a dictator, established a kingdom ruled by a military elite (Davis 1928).

The country was reunited in 1820, under another *mulatto*, Boyer. He occupied the Dominican Republic from 1822 to 1844. His Presidency was followed by a succession of repressive governments, which usually ended in bloody revolts following the original class/color and regional cleavages. At that time, Haiti was virtually isolated from the rest of the world; it was shunned by slave holding countries, and its economy was in shambles. Its independence was ultimately recognized by France in 1825, and by the United States in 1862 (Leyburn 1966).

In 1915, the United States invaded Haiti. This was as much a political move as a move to rescue the country's fledgling economy. Several factors prompted this move: the United States wanted total supremacy in Latin America and would not tolerate, in accordance with the Monroe Doctrine, the intervention of foreign powers in the area. The American Government was also interested in securing rights to operate a naval station in Haiti. It needed to protect its investments in Haiti's sugar plantations, the National Railroad, and the National Bank. Finally, Germany's intentions to secure exclusive customs control of Haiti, as well as to secure rights to operate its own naval base on the island, threatened these plans (Davis 1968; Leyburn 1966; Logan 1968).

The American occupation of Haiti lasted until 1934. In the long run, it was not successful in resolving Haiti's political and economic problems. Some progress was made in consolidating the economy, improving the country's standard of living, rebuilding Haiti's institutions and, improving health and

agricultural systems. However, the Americans' failure
to understand the roots of Haiti's social problems,
their "..brusque attempt to plant democracy there by
drill and harrow" (US Dept. of State Report in Logan
1968:140), and their determination to set up a class
system modeled on the American system backfired. Soon
after the Americans left in 1934, Haiti slid back to
its own political system regulated by revolutions.
The more lasting and beneficial effects of the occupation were unintended. They included a revival of
nationalistic feelings and an acknowledgment of their
African roots by the upper class.[16] The patriotic
movement united Haitians of all color and classes in a
common determination to end the occupation (Nicholls
1985; Davis 1967).

A series of governments followed, each terminated
by a revolution. Economic and cultural progress continued to be made with covert aid from the Americans.
Most of the heads of state continued to be from
Classes I and II, and no one sought to actively improve the lot of the masses. Duvalier came to power
in 1957. He was a Class III man, who had risen up the
social hierarchy by taking advantage of American-
introduced opportunities for social mobility through

education.   Duvalier was a shrewd and ruthless
politician.   He astutely called on the masses for support by appealing to their traditional religion,
vodou, and their folk heroes such as the *marrons*.
Duvalier also sought the support of the urban and
rural populations.   He consolidated his hold by em-
phasizing the oppositions between the social
categories and attacking the elite's own traditional
power base: their control over the nation's economic
and political institutions.   He systematically reduced
the power of the major groups and institutions, such
as the Army and the Catholic Church.   His handling of
noiriste[17] rhetoric appealed to Class III members, but
had little influence among Class IV.   He was able to
maintain power and snuff out opposition through the
use of a well-armed private militia, the *tonton*
macoutes.   With the exodus of professionals and educated elite came the breakdown of governmental in-
frastructures.   Agricultural production plunged, foreign investments were withdrawn, and once more the
country returned to isolation.   Duvalier gave himself
the title of "President for Life"; at his death his
son inherited the title.   Jean-Claude's regime was
different in many respects.   He faced the opposition

of several dissatisfied groups; "tensions between
noiriste politicians and *macoute* leaders on the one
hand and younger technocrats recruited in more recent
years, who were less committed to Duvalierist ideology, on the other" (Nicholls 1985). Jean-Claude
lacked the astuteness of his father, and his understanding of the dynamics of Haitian social structure
and class oppositions. He formed alliances in Classes
I and II and ultimately lost touch with Class III
(Nicholls 1985; Diederich and Burt 1969; Lundahl
1979). It is still too early to analyze the dynamics
that brought the Duvalier regime to an end in February
1986, and to evaluate the changes that this long dic-
tatorship may have brought. However, after almost 30
years of near isolation, the outlook is grim. Oppositions and hierarchy remain, and the lot of the masses
has certainly not improved. They once again had
merely been used for "ulterior motives".

The roots of Haiti's traditional pattern of active
migration can be traced to this history of poor
economic policies, social oppositions, the legitima-
tion of hierarchy, and political instability.

CLASS STRUCTURE, RURAL-URBAN OPPOSITIONS

This section presents an overview of social organization among the rural and urban groups. The urban-rural distinction entails more than locality and class differentiation. It reflects the European and African heritages that infuse every aspect of Haitian social organization and culture. Although social distance is maintained between the categories, any one of them cannot be examined without taking into consideration its place within the larger picture of Haitian society.

Members of Classes I and II dominate all government and national institutions, are professionals, Christian, and generally never engage in manual labor. They reside in urban centers, are wealthy, and well-educated. They speak French, but also Haitian Creole. Although they only comprise 5% of the population, they control the country's economy. They are engineers, physicians, lawyers, bankers, and monopolize the import-export market. In sharp contrast, the rural population (Class IV), usually referred to as *peyizan* (peasants), or *moun en deyò* (people from hinterland), is poor, attached to the land, practice mainly *vodou*,

is monolingual in Creole, and largely illiterate.
Both groups also differ in their social organization.
Whereas urban social institutions are patterned after
the Western European system, rural ones reflect
stronger African influences (Leyburn 1966; Metraux
1960; Lundahl 1979; Comhaire-Sylvain 1959, 1961).

In rural areas, the family (*fanmi*) is the basic
ritual and socio-economic unit. Extended families often live on inherited land in clusters of *kay* (houses)
called *lakou* or yard, homestead. *Lakou* may be
clustered in small villages or isolated among fields.
Members of the extended family all share rights in inherited land.   Because of the pattern of inheritance
that prescribes that male and female offsprings inherit equally from their father and their mother, the
size of parcels owned individually has been greatly
reduced over the years. Plots are usually scattered,
making it hard for the farmer to work efficiently.
This, together with the fact that productivity is down
due to overfarming and that population density has increased, contribute to the poor conditions which
prevail in Haiti's rural areas (Leyburn 1966; Metraux
1960; Lundahl 1979; Comhaire-Sylvain 1959, 1961).

The Haitian rural family is made of individuals linked by bilateral, as well as a variety of fictitious kinship ties. As a self-contained unit, the family regulates the lives of its members, and major decisions regarding them are made inside the family. Together they take care of problems outside the family (Fjellman and Gladwin 1985; Larose 1978; Laguerre 1978). Richman (1984:57) notes that Haitians differentiate between different kinds of persons according to their area of origin. She refers to what Haitians call "*mentalite lakou*, literally, 'the yard mentality', (which) also describes the Haitian distrust of anyone who is from outside the compound, where the extended family traditionally resides."

Members of a *lakou* share reciprocal economic and ritual obligations, they form a *nasyon*, a lineage. An informant described *nasyon* as

> a big family. One reckons his/her
> *nasyon* from the mother or the father's
> side. In general, all who belong
> together share the same substance, the
> same blood.

Therefore, individuals belong to more than one *nasyon* or lineage. This term is also used to describe a family of *vodou* spirits that share similar characteristics. For the rural Haitian, the land, the

spirits, the ancestors, and kin are linked. On the
lakou is the lineage's *demanbre*, where ancestral
spirits reside. My informant said that it is where
the family's first *lakou* was established,

> manman ou mouri la, papa ou mouri la, ou
> antere yo la, laҟou sa-a rele yon
> demanbre. Toujou gen yon moun ki rete
> la. (your mother died there, your father
> died there, you buried them there, this
> *lakou* is called the *demambre*. Someone
> from the family always lives there).
> Even if one is the last from his/her
> line and moves away to start his/her own
> *lakou*, he/she always holds on to the
> original *lakou*. Vodouists have to go
> back to the original family *lakou* for
> special services once a year. A special
> tree is planted on the *lakou* for the
> family *lwa* (spirits). In case someone
> is not vodouist and has a *demambre* on
> his land, he should find a *vodou* prac-
> titioner to care for it.

Individuals may also have links with others in
different locations for different purposes. For example, farmers may form *sosyete* or *kombit* teams
(corvee) to help each other in special cases: during
harvests, to build a boat, clear a new field. These
are reciprocal obligations and members of a *kolonn*
(file) keep track of their own obligations. The individual holding a *kombit* provides food, beverage, and
music for the workers. A special drum beat provides
the tempo for the *kolonn*.

Common-law unions or *plasaj* are most common among the rural population, and polygamy is widely prac- ticed. A man can have several *plase* (common-law spouses) on different plots of land, and several children to work them. A woman, on the other hand, is expected to remain faithful to her *plase*. Both parties are bound by specific sets of rights, duties, and obligations sanctioned by the community. A *plasaj* can be broken at any time by either party, and most unions that end up in marriages (sanctioned by a Christian church) started as *plasaj*. Offspring from *plasaj* unions are often recognized as legal children of their fathers (Lowenthal 1984; Comhaire-Sylvain 1958, 1961).

There is a division of labor according to gender. Men and women have distinct spheres of activities. Land is always worked by men; the management of a farm is a man's business. *"Gason sekle, plante, deplate. Fi rekolte, l'al van"* (men weed, plant, clear new fields. Women help during harvest and sell). Women are entrepreneurs; "the market is a woman's garden", says a Haitian proverb. Women usually lease out their

share of inherited land and use the proceeds as capital for the rental of market stalls. It is also customary at marriage for a man to give his wife enough
cash to help her get started in business. While the
husband takes care of long term expenditures, such as
acquisition of land and fertilizers, the wife assumes
the largest share of household expenses, including
those related to her children's education (Nicholls
1985; Mintz 1960, 1971; Legerman 1962; Locher 1975).

The *lakou-plasaj* system allows men more
flexibility to work scattered plots and gives women
more freedom to carry on their commerce. A Haitian
market woman leads a semi-nomadic life. She spends an
average of three days a week traveling great distances
to regional markets, often bringing back goods for
sale locally. During her absence, other women help
care for her children and the father may also assume
some of these responsibilities.

The literature (Mintz 1959, 1966, 1971) and my own
observation show that rural Haitian women are astute
traders and their role in the national economy is invaluable. Although the system affords a Haitian woman
a great deal of flexibility, there are limits to the

extent of her opportunities. Implicit in the male-
female relationship are the hierarchical relationships
between land-trade and external-internal. Land that
is owned and worked by men is more valued than woman's
trade, and while internal trade is in the hands of
women, men control the more lucrative export market
(sugar, coffee, cotton, etc.).

By contrast, among the upper classes of urban centers, nuclear families are predominant, and religious
or civil marriages are the norm. "Family" is still an
important concept; one's family name and area of
origin represent one's position in the class hierarchy. Classes I and II are endogamous; they either in-
termarry or choose partners outside of Haiti. Most of
their members belong to the Catholic Church, which
used to be the official religion.[18] They claim to be
ignorant of *vodou* which they associate with the uneducated masses. Deren (1953: 15) notes that

> In the largest cities, and particularly
> in Port-au-Prince, the 'middle' and
> 'upper classes', influenced, no doubt,
> by conventional criteria of 'civilized'
> cultures, as well as the pressure of the
> Catholic Church, have altogether aban-
> doned Voudoun in favor of Christianity.
> The schism between these classes and the
> masses of the people is so great that
> the former are largely ignorant of
> Voudoun.

Those belonging to Classes I and II govern the country, and represent it in all its economic, social and political contacts with the world. They are well-educated and speak French. Some complete their education in foreign countries; for them, France is still the intellectual center. French Geography, History, and Literature are taught as part of the curriculum in all secondary schools.

The emerging Class III, "sandwiched" between the elite (Classes I and II), and the peasants (Class IV), reflects values and attributes from both groups. It is involved in a process of upward mobility that includes the appropriation of upper class markers (Lundahl 1985). "Class III people are a heterogeneous group. One of their outstanding characteristics is the extreme care which they take with the education of their children" (Comhaire-Sylvain 1959: 184). *Plasaj* is still practiced, although monogamy and church sanctioned marriages are more emphasized. Family ties and the concept of the family as a lineage is still very strong. Residential patterns tend to differ from the rural environment to the urban environment. There are few *lakou* in cities, but ties to area of origin and kinsmen are very strong (Leyburn 1966; Laguerre 1978,

1978b; Larose 1978). Among this group, the meaning of
nasyon has lost its restrictive connotation of family
as tribe. *Nasyon* means the Haitian people (*pèp
Ayisyen*), or an ethnic group, "*gen plysiè nasyon o
Zetazini*" (there are many ethnic groups in the United
States).

Informal networks based on further oppositions and
hierarchical relations, such as patron-client
relationships, cross-cut class boundaries. A *patron*
in high places is invaluable to an individual moving
to the city. The *patron* helps the client, or *moun pa*,
find jobs; "gives the client a break". In return,
this relationship adds to the patron's status in the
community. The *moun pa* offers loyalty by asking the
patron to be godfather to an offspring, or by bringing
offerings of produce, for example. Patron-client
relationships are also developed among Haitian immigrants in the United States.

In this category (Class III), religious affiliation and language use best reflect a series of
paradoxes brought about by conflicts arising between
tradition and aspirations. There is a wide range of
variation in religious practices and affiliation in
Class III. Many remain Catholic (most Haitians are

baptized in the Catholic Church), while others opt for conversion to Protestant Churches for a variety of reasons. Some perceive conversion as a way to distance themselves more radically from their peasant background because "Protestantism has been able to insist, more clearly, upon its incompatibility with Voudoun. Indeed, to the Voudoun serviteurs, there is a far greater incompatibility between the two branches of Christianity than there is between the Catholics and themselves" (Deren 1953 : 57). This stems from the fact that *vodou* is a syncretization of African religions, American Indian beliefs, and Catholicism. Some who renounce *vodou* practices (*"pa sèvi lwa"*: do not serve the spirits), and convert to *levangil* (Protestantism), often retain some attachment to *vodou* beliefs (Smucker 1984). An informant said that his family's *lwa* returned *amba d'lo* (under the water, where all spirits reside) since his grandfather died. Everyone in the *lakou* is now *levangil* and there is no one left to take care of them. Another said that certain traditions should be maintained. For example, one should still *"de'pose' yon boutèy kle'ren oubyen yon chandel"* (leave a bottle of raw rum or a candle) for the spirits, and even if *"sèvis mò* (services for the dead) are no longer held; in January one should pay respect to ancestors, like pouring coffee at the head of the grave for those who used to drink coffee".

Comhaire-Sylvain (1959) comments that in some Class III neighborhoods of Port-au-Prince, there is a high percentage of French speakers who "display a distinct preference for Creole at home and at work" (1959: 185). This practice reflects a belief that within the Haitian hierarchical system, literacy and the ability to speak French are attributes of upper classes. Thus, in order to move up the social ladder, an individual should acquire these markers (Hoffman 1984; Lundahl 1985).

The choice of language to be used in particular situations indicates social standing, degree of education, and the topic being discussed, as well as the status of those involved in the conversation. In general, formal discussions (those of a political, judiciary, educational etc. nature) are held in French. Creole is used in informal situations, among friends, or between a superior and an inferior. Within their linguistic repertoire, members of Classes I, II, and III have access to both languages, as well as to a number of levels within each language. Others

(Class IV), are restricted to varieties of Creole
ranging from forms of rural or *gros Creole*, regional
variations, or urban and gallicized Creoles. Gallicizing is a strategy by which individuals possessing
marginal knowledge of French can display their
familiarity with that language by using French phonol-
ogy and adding French endings to Creole words. In
this context, class differences, as well as education,
find their expression in language itself. Code-
switching, i.e switching from one language to another
within the same conversation, is a way of displaying
both one's performance and competence in a variety of
linguistic forms.[19] Thus, literacy and acquisition of
French are important elements of strategies of upward
mobility (Valdman 1984; Stewart 1968; Lofficiel 1968).

Several social factors contribute to emigration of
rural and urban poor Haitians. Members of the urban
Class III, who start a process of upward mobility but
find their efforts thwarted by unsurmountable class
and economic barriers, feel that emigration is the
only option open to them. Economic pressures are more
acute in the rural areas where population density,
land scarcity, and lack of employment opportunities in

other sectors force individuals to look elsewhere for
survival.

CHAPTER III

MIGRATION HISTORY

Haitian migration should be studied within the
context of the larger Caribbean migratory movement.
Since the 15th century, the Caribbean Basin has been
the site of intensive population movements. Whereas
the immigration flow used to be directed towards the
Caribbean basin, the pattern is now reversed. Currently the area is experiencing large scale intra and
extra-regional population flows (Sutton 1975; Kritz
1981). Kritz remarks that in the Caribbean Basin

> several conditions are present which
> stimulate new and reinforce existing
> migration flows: sharp, and in many
> cases, growing economic inequalities
> within and between countries; borders
> that are relatively uncontrolled and
> easy to cross; political conditions in
> many countries which stimulate
> emigration; sharp differences between
> contiguous countries in population
> growth and density; well-established
> transportation routes and systems that
> can be utilized at a cost that is within
> the economic means of a growing propor-
> tion of people in the region; and social
> networks, resulting from previous migra-
> tions, that extend across national
> boundaries, linking families and com-
> munities into transnational communica-
> tion and support systems (p.209).

Although the trends and patterns described by Kritz apply to the Caribbean region in general, the factors shaping each country's participation in the migratory movement are quite different. Historical, ecological, economic, demographic and political variables vary widely within the area and give each country a special profile.

There are several differences between the patterns of migration of Haitians of urban origins and those from rural areas. These variations reflect socio-economic, as well as urban-rural differences. Although both populations have a history of migration, their goals, destinations, reasons for migration, methods and strategies differ. The upper class has kept contact with France (considered by many to be a cultural parent), and have traveled extensively to the United States and Europe; many of its members have been educated overseas. The rural and urban poor populations, who have been culturally and educationally isolated, were kept from participating in politics and economic decisions. Attachment to the land was accompanied by lack of formal skills, absence of knowledge of the French language, and limited geographic and social mobility.

There have been several waves of intensive upper class migrations in Haiti's history. These can usually be linked to periods of political unrest or economic crises (Fontaine 1976:113). Jean-Batiste Point du Sable, the founder of Chicago, was a mulatto born in Saint Domingue and educated in Paris. He came to the United States in the 1770's, at the beginning of the Haitian War of Independence, immediately before American Independence was proclaimed (Laguerre 1984:161). A number of upper class Haitians left their country during the American occupation of the thirties. Their descendants are now integrated in communities in the United States, Canada, and in various countries in Latin America and Europe. Upper class emigration continued on a small scale until Duvalier came to power in 1957, and reached a peak in the early 60's. Most of the educated and profes- sionals who left the country at that time went to large industrial centers in France, Canada, Europe, francophone Africa - mainly Zaire - and the United States. For the most part, these early immigrants settled into white-collar positions (Laguerre 1984; Allman 1982).

In the mid-60's, migrants from the urban Class III settled predominantly in New York City, and to a lesser extent, in other Northeastern cities like Boston and Philadelphia, while some went as far West as Chicago. A large number migrated to Canada, mainly to Montreal and Quebec City. Although migration rates to the United States accelerated in the 60's and 70's, it was not until the late 70's that the influx of Haiti's rural migrants reached the United States (Laguerre 1984; Bastide 1974; Dejean 1978; Allman 1982).

Rural migration is not a new phenomenon in Haiti; it has been a viable strategy for those living in rural areas since the 19th century. Over the years, the distances traveled, the countries of destination, and the length of stay outside of Haiti have changed. Migrants from this category (Class IV), usually have little or no formal education, speak mainly Creole and are unskilled. Their background has seriously limited their chances for successful adaptation in the societies where they settle. Since this study is mainly concerned with problems related to rural and urban poor migration, a brief overview of the history of this process will serve to contextualize the problems that these immigrants face in the United

States.   The following section examines previous
Haitian migrations to neighboring countries, such as
Cuba, Santo Domingo and the Bahamas.

HAITIANS IN CUBA

Earliest reports of Haitian laborers in Cuban
fields date back to August 1900, when an appeal was
made to local planters and mining companies to stop
the importation of "contract labor from Haiti, Jamaica
and Turks Island, whence had come over a thousand
Negroes since January, 1900" (Perusek 1984:8).   The
opening of the sugar industry, mostly by American investors, at the turn of the century presented growers
with a dilemma. The potential for a lucrative trade
existed: the demand for sugar was increasing and the
land readily available, but while there was a shortage
of labor, immigration of non-whites was forbidden. In
1902, the United States and Cuba signed a Reciprocity
Treaty that guaranteed that Cuba would be the sole
foreign supplier of sugar to the U.S., and that in
return, the U.S. would receive this sugar at a
favorable rate.   A campaign to attract immigrants of
European descent to Cuba was largely unsuccessful, and

the predominantly Spanish   population who responded was not interested in doing farmwork.   The shortage of labor became so acute that in 1913, the Cuban Government allowed the importation of a restricted number of contract black workers from Haiti, Jamaica and other Caribbean countries.   Since the demand for manpower far exceeded the government quota and the sugar industry was booming, illegal aliens were overlooked and tolerated (Diaz 1973; Palmieri 1980).

This situation continued until the sugar market crashed in 1921. Sugar prices fell from 22.5c./lb. in 1920, to .2c./lb in 1921, and wages from a peak of $5.00/day to a mere .40c./day after 1921 (Perusek 1984).   By that time a stable migration pattern had been established. Between 1915 and 1921, 81,000 Haitians and 75,000 Jamaicans had entered Cuba both as legal and illegal workers.   Not all the workers returned home at the end of the season.   It is estimated that about one-third remained in Cuba. Despite the tumble of the sugar industry and the subsequent decrease in labor demand, Haitian laborers still came to Cuba. In 1937, Batista's government, responding to pressures from Cuban workers, ordered the deportation of thousands of Haitian immigrants and closed the country to them (Leyburn 1941:271).

Diaz (1973:32) notes that during fieldwork conducted in 1962, in Guanamaca, Cuba (a community of seasonal farm laborers largely populated by Haitian workers), he met Haitian immigrants who had entered Cuba illegally as late as 1950. These immigrants' homebase is in the Eastern portion of the island near the sugarcane fields. At the end of the sugar cane season most of these workers migrate to take part in the coffee harvest. Some of these immigrants had been in Cuba as early as 1915. They had come to Cuba with the intention of staying long enough to save money and then go home. Due to a variety of circumstances (new families, lack of money to finance a trip home and back, fear of losing whatever work they had), they never returned to Haiti. They live in isolated communities and have not been assimilated into Cuban society (Diaz 1973).

HAITIANS IN THE DOMINICAN REPUBLIC

The Dominican Republic has long been a major receiver of Haitian laborers. Next to the United

States, it still has the largest number of Haitian immigrants (Allman 1982). The Dominican Republic has
long been a major receiver of Haitians; both as
laborers and as immigrants. As mentioned earlier the
two countries were united between 1822 and 1844.
However, it was not until the early 1900's that a
steady influx of Haitian seasonal workers was established. As in the case of Cuba, this influx of
Haitian workers coincided with the increase of
American capital in the Dominican sugar industry. The
workers were tolerated only because there was a
shortage of farm laborers. Several attempts were made
to stem the rate of illegal migration by closing the
frontier. This strategy was difficult to enforce. Until recently, the frontier was not officially defined
and is even now far from being impenetrable. The
migration rate slowed down temporarily following the
ruthless murder of "up to 25,000 Haitians by the dictator Trujillo in 1937" (Perusek 1984:13). At that
time there were approximately 60,000 Haitians living
in the Dominican Republic (Leyburn 1941:271).

Although the two countries have not been on
friendly terms, the clandestine and illegal traffic of
Haitian workers continues to this day under the tacit

understanding of both governments (Allman 1982; Bajeux 1973). The illicit traffic of illegal Haitian workers benefits both governments: the Dominican growers, who profit from cheap labor; and the Haitians who send much needed remittances home, thus alleviating the economic situation in the countryside.   Kritz (1981:232) notes that Haiti encourages emigration as a means of obtaining foreign exchange and increasing its revenue.

As in Cuba, there is little contact between the immigrant population and the host society.   Although Haitian workers are essential to the Dominican sugar industry, they are ruthlessly exploited and made to live and work under conditions hardly better than slavery (Allman 1982; Bajeux 1973).

HAITIANS IN THE BAHAMAS

Most rural, impoverished Haitians, who left Haiti during Duvalier's government, tried to stay as close as possible to home and went either to the Bahamas, French Guyana, Martinique or Guadeloupe.   With the meagre resources at their disposal, and the pressing need to find new sources of employment, the Bahamas

was a logical choice for emigrants of rural and urban
poor backgrounds. The Haitians could still make the
trip clandestinely by boat, enter the country un-
detected, and then join underground communities.
Haitian migration to the Bahamas was negligible until
1957, when "the migration trickle increased to what
the Immigration Department considered to be a `flood'"
(Marshall 1979:99).   About the same time, 1958, the
economic situation in the Bahamas worsened.   In
response to a recession in the United States, tourism,
the major source of employment in the Bahamas, suffered a severe setback. Bahamian seasonal farm
laborers in the United States had to come home, due to
major crop failures there. Unemployment became a
serious problem.   Still, illegal Haitian immigration
continued. The "Haitian problem" became the "Haitian
flood".   According to Marshall (1979), the Bahamian
Deputy Prime Minister estimated that close to 40,000
Haitians were living in the Bahamas in 1973, while she
quotes the Chief Immigration Officer's estimate of
25,000 for 1970, up from 10,000 in January 1963
(Bahamian Immigration Department), and 30,000 in September of the same year, according to the former
Haitian Consul.   An official census of the island's

population indicated that there were 6,151 Haitians
holding legal work permits in the country in 1970, as
compared to 4,170 for 1963. These figures underline
the magnitude of the illegal migratory movement of
Haitian peasants and poor urban dwellers.

In a statement which brings back flashes of the
Cuban and Dominican experiences of unwanted illegal
Haitians, Marshall (1979:xvii) notes "that in this
isolation of a possible 40,000 people, or 23 per cent
of the total Bahamian population, there lies a great
potential for unrest". The Bahamian government has
been dealing with "the Haitian problem" actively since
1957. Responding to pressures from its population, it
has instated an active program of interception, incarceration and deportation. In 1980, a deadline of
January 18, 1981 was issued for all illegal Haitians
to leave the country (Allman 1982:10). Attempts to
involve the Haitian government in the resolution of
this crisis have been unsuccessful. Again, as in the
case of Cuba and the Dominican Republic, it seems that
the Haitian government is either insensitive to the
plight of Haitian illegal immigrants, or turns a deaf
ear because this illegal migration is both a way of
solving the unemployment and overpopulation problems,

as well as providing a source of income for the
country's weakened economy.

In an effort to remain invisible and avoid deportation, the immigrants have formed underground communities, avoid any contact with the local population,
shun health and educational facilities, and thus per-
petuate the cycle of poverty, illiteracy and exploita-
tion. As in the case of the Haitian immigrant communities of Cuba and the Dominican Republic, Haitians
in the Bahamas have maintained their ethnic identity
by isolating themselves from their host societies, by
being excluded from the economic and political power
centers, and by maintaining links with their home communities. Marshall notes that "the illegal nature of
the Haitian migration increases not only the need for
isolation, but also the difficulties involved in
breaching this isolation" (Marshall 1979:127). Assimilation under these conditions becomes a virtually
impossible process. Marshall (p.207) wonders how long
this situation can last if efforts are not made to
bridge economic and cultural gaps.

As Marshall explains so vividly, "the Haitian
peasant migrated illegally because he possesses none
of the attributes which would make him a desirable

immigrant" (1979:xvii); he is thus constrained to take unskilled, low paying, menial jobs. Haitian peasants went to the Bahamas attracted by reports that a booming tourist industry was creating a great number of jobs. But once more the lack of formal job skills, as well as poor command of the English language, prevented most Haitians from getting these jobs. Since the Bahamian economy relies mainly on tourism, and agriculture is poorly developed, the opportunities for farm work are limited. The already high unemployment rate among unskilled Bahamian nationals renders the competition for casual labor even more intense. Where in the Dominican Republic the Haitian laborer is needed, albeit resented, in the Bahamas he does not even have the advantage of occupying that niche, however poorly paid.

The Bahamian migration introduced other factors into the process. Distances, cost, and government regulations make return trips home more difficult. Thus the original character of rural migration has had to change. It is no longer a seasonal or temporary movement: although immigrants still plan to return home after accumulating enough savings, their economic

situation makes that prospect increasingly more difficult to contemplate. In many cases it ends up being
a permanent move.   Furthermore, the Bahamian
government's campaign to expel Haitian immigrants has
led the Haitians to search even further north for
sources of employment, and "rather than return to
Haiti, most of them fled to Florida, stacked like
cordwood in ramshackle sailboats" (Bogue 1979: 9).

It is with the closing of the Bahamian outlet to
rural Haitians, and the mass arrival of Haitian illegal aliens - also known as boat people - to Southern
Florida, that the presence of Haitian immigrants in
the United States became a "public problem". But
Haitians, like other Caribbeans, had been migrating to
the United States in small numbers for quite some
time. The latest Haitian wave of immigration, which
peaked between 1978 and 1981, coincided with the Cuban
"Mariel boat lift" (the wave of Cubans who arrived in
the United States by boat). In a way, it completed a
cycle. With the arrival of Haitians from rural and
urban poor backgrounds, there is now in the United
States a representative cross-section of Haitian
society.

HAITIAN IMMIGRANT COMMUNITIES IN THE UNITED STATES

The United States is the largest receiver of Haitian emigrants. Laguerre (1984:160) identifies three main waves of Haitian emigration to the United States. Between 1791 and 1803, refugees from the Haitian revolution - colonists, mulattos and slaves - settled in New Orleans, Charleston, New York, and Boston. A second wave of emigration took place during the American occupation of Haiti (1915-1934). Those refugees settled in New York, mainly in Harlem. The third wave started in the late 50's (Fontaine 1976:113). Most of the Haitian immigrants in the U.S. arrived after 1957, when Franscois Duvalier came to power. The last two waves coincided with periods that "have been characterized by extreme use of coercion, considerable inroads by foreign economic interests, and above all by grievous despoliation of the peasantry" (Fontaine 1976:113). The majority of the early arrivals came from Classes I and II. They were intellectuals and professionals, who fled mainly for political reasons. They formed small communities in large industrial cities and settled most often into white-collar jobs. Later on, members of Class III

also left, as it was becoming increasingly difficult
for them to make a living - the political climate in
Haiti was stifling the economy and eroding the freedom
of individuals. These immigrants settled in New York
City, in Boston, Washington, D.C. and Chicago.

In addition to the Haitian immigrants legally admitted in the United States, there is a sizable
population of illegal aliens. Because of this illegal
component, accurate data on the size of the Haitian
immigrant population are hard to compile. Some illegal immigrants come with a tourist or student visa,
and when such visas expire, may elect either to apply
for immigrant visas, marry an American citizen, or
join the underground illegal community. All live in
fear of being arrested and sent back home. It used to
be possible for parents of children born in this
country to be allowed to remain in the U.S. to care
for these children; this is no longer true. Haitians
who can afford to come to this country using the above
strategies are usually urban dwellers with at least
several years of education and formal skills (Buchanan
1979; Laguerre 1984).

HAITIAN COMMUNITY IN NEW YORK CITY

The Haitian community of New York City is the oldest and by far the largest Haitian community in the United States. Unlike smaller communities - Boston, Philadelphia, Miami - it contains immigrants from all social backgrounds and economic statuses. [The New York Haitian community is of interest to this study because it mirrors both the dynamic relationship that exists between social categories in Haiti, and il-lustrates how these dynamics are affected by pressures from American society.] In the Haitian community of New York, several kinds of strategies of adaptation are used by immigrants of rural and urban poor origins. These strategies are influenced by the so-cial composition of the community, as well as by other external factors.

Traditionally, New York City has been the Mecca of Caribbean migration to the United States; "in the folklore, gossip, and even geography lessons of the peoples of the region the image of the City is preg-nant with marvel, mystery, and myth" (Bryce-Laporte 1979:216). It has been used as an entrepot from which migrants later fan out to other destinations. A high proportion of the Caribbean population of New York City, and therefore of Haitians, is made up of illegal and undocumented aliens.   Statistics on the size of this population are hard to compile; "the exact figures for illegal immigrants in the United States are often speculative and believed to be gravely exaggerated for political and special reasons" (idem:218).

Laguerre (1984:31) estimates that in 1984, there were roughly 450,000 legal and illegal immigrants of Haitian extraction in New York City, most of whom arrived after 1965.   They come from all sectors of Haitian society, from urban as well as rural areas. In a way, this ethnic community mirrors Haitian social and cultural diversity; it reflects and strives to recreate the social and structural divisions of the mother country.

Because of their color, Haitian immigrants are relegated together with Black Americans and other people of color to the lowest strata of American society.   Dominguez (1975:29) notes that in the American class structure, color and social status have become synonymous with ethnic identity.   She claims that this situation is a carry-over from the days of slavery.   In colonial times, Africans, as a racial group, were forced to acquire a new identity and a new status - that of black and slave - despite their individual "tribal" and ethnic characteristics. In modern American society, the status of slave has been translated into the lowest social class. Afro-Americans and any other groups of individuals of Negro background are automatically given this identity and status. Immigrants of mixed ancestry are at a loss in this system. Whereas discrimination in Latin America and the Caribbean is based primarily on rank or sociocultural position, in the United States "the factor of race operates so that locality, class, or ethnic differences are minor in comparison" (Green 1975: 84). Most of these immigrants do not perceive themselves as Blacks, because Haitian society in particular - and Caribbean societies in general - recognize "intermediate racial categories (such as *mulatto*, *indio*, and *trigueno* in Spanish) whose members are granted relatively higher status than `Negros' (i.e. blacks)" (Dominguez 1975: 31). In an effort to set themselves apart from Black Americans and preserve their unique culture, Haitians draw on their ethnic differences: their French cultural links, the Creole language and their comportment (see Buchanan 1979, 1983; Dominguez 1975; Fontaine 1976; Laguerre 1984).

Under the apparent veil of homogeneity attributed to it, the Haitian community of New York City is segmented into social categories and hierarchies patterned after the Haitian system. Buchanan (1983:10) states that the "model of" reality that Haitians bring to this country is composed of social categories distinguished on the basis of wealth, family name, ancestry, education, comportment and color. It is then used as a "model for" reality by the Haitian community. But objective reality, in the form of new socioeconomic, structural and cultural factors within the United States, impinge on this model and preclude its application. Adaptive strategies have then had to be devised in order to cope with these changes. According to Buchanan (1979), this situation generates conflicts that are expressed in controversies over language use (French vs. Haitian Creole) among members of the community, and over choice of residential area. Just as language use serves as a class marker in Haitian society, in New York City it has become the vehicle through which conflicts over class membership and social status are negotiated within the community.

/ Although the Haitian community of New York City is internally polarized by class, economic, social and political divisions, it is learning to set aside its traditional oppositions and to act as a unified group in order to solve its problems and promote its political interests.

Conditions of life in New York City affect and limit the ways in which the Haitian community structures itself. The niches that Haitian immigrants have been forced to occupy often do not correspond to the social statuses they had at home. Limitations, such as mastery of English, level of education, skills, and legal status in the United States, affect the position of immigrants in American society and within the Haitian community. Socioeconomic factors, imposed by the host community, generate undercurrents of tension within the Haitian community between those who have achieved economic superiority and higher standards of living, and those who rely on the ascribed statuses they had at home. Some members of Classes I and II have been successful in finding work in their field. Others, hampered by the lack of useful or transferable skills and a poor knowledge of English, had to settle for low paying, low status jobs. On the other hand, some Haitians from Class III have been able to obtain well-paying jobs as blue-collar workers and find themselves better off financially than Haitians of Classes I and II.

Unskilled, illiterate, and illegal immigrants of urban poor and rural origins find it difficult to adapt in the big city, and unemployment among this group is very high (Buchanan 1979,1983; Laguerre 1984). There is little or no hope of upward mobility for these immigrants, even though in some cases their economic situation has improved. Within the community, they are still regarded as "*moun mòn*" or "*moun sòt*" (i.e. illiterate, backward people). The only way out of their predicament is to work diligently and see that through education, their children will have a chance for a better future.

Immigrants who can speak English have access to better jobs and for them, assimilation into American society is easier. All immigrants realize that access to, and the ability to speak English is one of the keys to success in America. Therefore, just as the command of French underlies social divisions in Haitian society, knowledge of English is becoming the basis of social cleavages within the community and an important factor in the adaptive process.

Even as economic opportunity is helping to level and bridge class differences, other factors are brought into the social identity negotiation process within the community. Ancestry, place of origin, behavior, and level of education become symbols of one's true class identity, and the choice of which neighborhood to settle in and which members of the community to associate with become important decisions. In fact, says Laguerre, "the territorial space occupied by the immigrants is more or less divided along class lines that are determined by their previous class positions in the Haitian political economy and the length of time they have lived in New York" (1984:50). Buchanan (1983) notes that most Haitian immigrants reside in the same neighborhoods as Black Americans, Hispanics, and other people of Caribbean origins. Neighborhoods are rated according to the kind of people who live in them. At first, Haitians settled in Brooklyn. Over the years, as their economic situations improved, they moved out. Queens and some areas of Brooklyn attract immigrants from the middle class who are better educated and better off financially.

Wealthier Haitians tend to settle in Nassau and Westchester counties.

Adaptation to their new environment is a complex process for Haitian immigrants. It takes time to acquire a good understanding of the City, the community, the job market, "to figure out the system" and be part of a network. Ethnic networks are useful in helping one to find a place to live, a job, and to learn one's way in the city. Catholic and Protestant churches play a vital role in the community. They provide spiritual as well as emotional and financial support to their members. *Vodou* is widely practiced among Haitians in New York and services are held periodically (Laguerre 1984:58-61).

Several Haitian community centers offer a variety of support services, as well as cultural and educational programs. They also act as advocates of Haitian interests in matters ranging from immigration policy and legislation, bilingual education, job training programs, and the development of food distribution to the needy. Haitian immigrant communities across the United States "have decided to join forces in a national network to work toward more meaningful and productive lives for Haitians in the U.S. and in

Haiti" (Haitian Centers Council Newsletter, Spring

1985). The network would become an umbrella organiza-

tion that would represent and safeguard the interests

of all Haitians, and work toward making the com-

munities more self-sufficient and less dependent on

outside financial support.

Immigration of rural Haitians to the United States

is a rather new phenomenon. Until the late 70's, only

a handful of Haitians of rural or urban poor origins

had come to this country. Between 1980, when the U.S.

government briefly relaxed its immigration policy, and

September 1981, when the INS instituted a new policy

of interdiction, hundreds of boats loaded with

refugees landed in Southern Florida. These immigrants

settled in the Miami area, and some have now moved to

other locations (Stepick 1984). Their legal status is

still unclear and until it is resolved, their future

in this country looks very bleak (see Appendix I).

The plight of this uneducated, unskilled, often

unemployed or underemployed population has attracted

the attention of the media towards Haitian immigrants

of all class backgrounds. This attention is not al-

ways welcomed by some immigrants of Classes I and II,

who resent being identified with Haitians of Classes III and IV.

These and other conflicts are also present among the Haitian immigrant communities in the migrant labor camps and in Rochester, New York. However, the social dynamics of these environments and the social composition of the communities influence the range, as well as the kinds of adaptive strategies used by the immigrants.

CHAPTER IV

FROM HAITI TO THE UNITED STATES:
AWAY FROM PERIPHERY TOWARD A CENTER

MIGRATION AND ADAPTATION

This chapter focuses on the migration and adaptation processes of Haitian boat people. It examines the reasons that prompt Haitians to migrate. It explores the ways in which Haitians make their choices, and the strategies they use to cope with their problems in the United States. Migration, I argue, is in itself a strategy to move from periphery to center. This chapter demonstrates that the 'boat people migration' is the logical development of an already well-established pattern. The factors preceding this migration wave, i.e. the closing of the Cuban, Dominican, and Bahamian markets to Haitian workers, have already been described in Chapter III. Adaptation is defined here as the way individuals learn to function in a different and new culture and society. It is a process over time, during which Haitian immigrants become part of American society, during which they have to learn new rules of social behavior. They

come to realize that rules of social conduct which applied in the Haitian context are not always valid in
the United States. Haitian immigrants often talk
about having to learn new ways of doing things.
Migrant farm workers, for example, have to learn how
to pick potatoes according to the way the farmer wants
them picked.   Immigrants also have to make choices
regarding their future and come to grips with the fact
that some of their expectations will not be realized.

I suggest that each Haitian immigrant has a vision
of a specific center that he/she wants to reach, an
idea of where he/she stands in the periphery, and some
form of strategic plan for reaching the center. The
perception of center and periphery is colored by the
immigrants' own experiences and backgrounds, and their
strategies for coping and making it are influenced by
their native cultural ideas. Faced with a different
set of social, economic, cultural and ecological factors, immigrants have to readjust their cultural com-
passes, their goals, and their strategies.

The process of adaptation includes a liminal
period during which immigrants are forging their new
identity, using elements from both their home and host
cultures. By liminality (see Van Gennep 1960), I mean

the period during which the immigrant is no longer only Haitian, but not yet Haitian-American. It is this liminal stage that is being investigated, the period when immigrants are involved in an interplay between their own cultural identities and assigned identities, imposed on them by the host society.

I suggest that a distinction can be made between social and cultural liminality.[20] Social liminality begins when the migrants make the decision to leave Haiti. It could be argued that this stage lasts until the immigrants' legal status in America is resolved, when they receive the coveted "green card" and become legally incorporated in American society. The duration of cultural liminality, on the other hand, varies with each individual. I propose that, at least for Haitian immigrants, it starts before they leave Haiti, as they detach themselves from the constraints of the home society. It continues as the immigrants learn to function in their new environment, each at his/her own pace. "Each immigrant has a double identity and a double vision, being suspended between an old and a new home, an old and a new self" (Grumwald 1985: 100). For some, cultural liminality never ends.

It is in this context that adaptation will be described: why Haitian immigrants decide to emigrate; where they choose to settle; how they deal, or cope with their problems; and the constraints within which they are forced to operate using their cultural background.   These constraints stem from the social reality of American society - such as its class structure, cultural, economic, legal systems - as well as the problems and limitations of the Haitian immigrants themselves - obligations and expectations from those at home, social class, historical background, education, experience, etc.

Even though migration experiences have not always been positive, Haitians of rural and urban poor backgrounds continue to choose migration as a viable strategy for survival. In some ways, the lives of Haitian immigrants are not very different from those of slaves, from the way in which they are recruited, the mode of transportation, the living quarters, and the kind of work they do, to the pay they receive. The presence of Haitian workers has often been considered a social problem for the host communities: the Cubans and the Dominicans did not want such a large black population in their midst; the Bahamians were

alarmed that, because of its size, the Haitian community (23% of the total Bahamian population) was a
potential source of internal disturbance. The
presence of Haitian workers has also been considered a
source of economic problems for the host countries:
Haitian workers received, and were content with, much
lower wages than their Cuban or Dominican counterpart,
and they were willing to accept work that no one else
was willing to do, under conditions that no one else
would tolerate.

MIGRATION THEORIES AND THE HAITIAN BOAT PEOPLE

Traditional migration theories look at the migration process in terms of "pull" and "push" factors,
operating in both the receiving and the sending
societies (Mc Donald and Mc Donald 1964; Philpott
1970; Sutton 1973; Bryce-Laporte 1979; Kritz 1981).
These approaches describe migrants as "rational cal-
culators," who search for the best opportunities and
the right time to leave their countries, in order to
maximize their gains. They also see the receiving
countries as "the dynamic agents which pull migrants
to them" (Perusek 1984:4). While these factors are

useful in understanding certain dynamics of migratory flows in general, they seem insufficient and inadequate to explain Haitian migration.

Certain "push factors" have been identified by migration theorists within the historical and contemporary contexts described in Chapter II. Perusek (1984) examines the history of Haitian migration, and observes that conditions in Haiti (mainly poverty), rather than in the receiving countries, influence the rate of migration. Even when the economic climate in the host countries becomes unfavorable (i.e. labor conditions in Cuba, the Dominican Republic and the Bahamas), "once a pattern of migration was established, it was conditions facing Haitians in Haiti which resulted in its continued stability" (1984:11). Leyburn (1941:269-270) claims that migration is one way that Haitians deal with overpopulation and the gradual and inexorable depletion of the land. Allman states that "external migration is clearly an important demographic phenomenon in Haiti" (1982:8), and that "the major factor controlling the flow of Haitians out of Haiti appears to be the barriers receiving countries erect to prevent them from entering" (idem:11). Fontaine notes that throughout

the course of Haitian history, "emigration has been
used as a safety valve in periods of crisis to allay
the pressures of economic, social, and political
demands which threaten to blow up the system"
(1976:126). Others, like Marshall, perceive that the
economic aspects of migration have been accorded too
much emphasis, and suggest that individual motiva-
tions, as well as environmental concerns, should also
be taken into consideration.

It is evident that some of the problems that contribute to Haitian migration have their roots in
Haitian history, while others depend to a lesser extent on external factors such as global economic
trends, labor demands in surrounding areas and political intervention by foreign powers. Following are
some of the internal factors that affect Haitian
migration:

1. Inheritance laws require the even division of
already small plots among all heirs. The roots of
this system can be found in Toussaint and Petion's
land distribution plan that fragmented the land and
discouraged the formation of large holdings, tied the
rural population to the land, and kept it out of the

mainstream of economic and political decisions (Leyburn 1966; 1971).

2. The continued success of Saint Domingue's labor intensive economy depended on a continuous supply of cheap manpower. Very large numbers of slaves were imported into the colony to work the land at a modest cost. While the French were aggressively exploiting their colony, Spain's holdings were floundering economically. The slave population in these colonies (e.g. Cuba, the Dominican Republic) never approximated that of Haiti. As a result, Haiti's population density is one of the highest in the Caribbean and in Latin America (Davis 1967; Lundahl 1979).

3. One of the legacies of the colonial system is the "two-caste" social structure described by Leyburn (1941). A small affluent educated minority holds the strings of economic and political power. The large majority is poorly educated and kept out of political and economic decisions. The American occupation fostered the development of a small middle class which is still vying for recognition and survival. Relations between these social categories are tense and antagonistic (Nicholls 1985).

4. Haiti has had a long history of political in-
stability and repression of individual liberties.
Politics and economics are inextricably mixed in Haiti
(Stepick 1984).

5. After Independence, fearful of losing its
autonomy, Haiti discouraged foreign investments while
the United States invested heavily in the sugar industry in Cuba and the Dominican Republic. It was not
until the occupation that Americans started investing
large sums in Haiti. The *cacos* (rebel group) mounted
attacks against the Americans to protest the occupation and the imposition of corvee work. Haitians
feared that the occupation was the first step toward
the re-establishment of slavery (Nicholls 1985; Bureau
of American Republics 1893).

While Haitian migration responded to the "pull" of
perceived opportunities elsewhere in the Caribbean,
Haitians were often victims of international economic
and political forces. A sharp drop in the price of
sugar on the international market brought about the
collapse of the Cuban sugar industry in 1921, and
larger economic and political concerns brought about
the American occupation of Haiti. The Bahamian labor
market was in great part affected by a drop in

tourism, which in turn was a result of a depression in the United States. And when it became more difficult for Haitians to migrate to the Bahamas, the emigrants headed for the next accessible and most advantageous place, the southern coast of Florida (Marshall 1979).

Thus I argue that in the Haitian case, there is no single cause for migration. The classic "push-pull" model does not take into consideration the cultural meaning of external migration for Haitians. For Haitians, migration is a culturally viable alternative. Migration is part of a social process, as well as being one of the ideas in a system of ideas that guide Haitians in everyday life. It is a culturally accepted strategy that Haitians can use in their movement from periphery to center.

Migration and adaptation, I argue, are closely linked. The adaptation process begins even before the migrants leave home. They gradually change focus and dissociate themselves from their environment, they project themselves into the future and a different environment, instead of looking for solutions within the constraints of their home society.

For the Haitian, the process of adaptation includes two sets of ideas. One is an idea of Haitian society and the ways in which problems are solved in this context. The other is an idea of American society that they construct from what they have learned from other immigrants and the image of America that is projected abroad. When the immigrants come in contact with the reality of American life, they have to readjust their perspectives, their goals, their way of approaching and solving problems. But these adjustments in turn are affected and influenced by Haitian cultural ideas and social structure.

HAITIAN BOAT PEOPLE

In the 70's, Haitians began arriving clandestinely in southern Florida, a few boats at a time carrying 20 or 30 people. By the late 70's, the frequency and size of the groups increased. This migration wave peaked in 1980, when Haitian immigrants, as well as Cuban refugees, arrived in droves. As the migration acquired momentum, local populations began to react defensively against both Haitians and Cubans. They resented the intrusion of these people in their state, the overload on their economy and social services agencies (Stepick 1984:1).

The immigrants arrived here in a variety of ways. Most came directly from Haiti, others already had prior migration experiences. They had been to the Bahamas and other countries along the Caribbean Basin, and a few had gone as far as Europe and Canada (Laguerre 1984; Allman and Richman 1985). While most members of that wave entered this country by boat, some arrived by plane on a tourist visa. One inform- ant had been to Belgium for two years before acquiring a permit to enter the United States, another had worked in French Guyana for several years before ar- riving in Florida.

MIGRATION PROCESS IN TWO SOCIAL CATEGORIES: URBAN AND RURAL

Using ethnographic data, this section presents the natives' point of view of the migration process, i.e. how Haitian immigrants perceived and described their experiences. For analytical purposes the migration process will be divided into three phases: migration, immigration, and resettlement.

Phase 1. Migration, "*kite peyi nou*" (leaving our country)

The migration phase deals mainly with the immigrants' perception of social "reality" in Haiti, how the system is structured, how it functions, and how far individuals can manipulate it. It includes the decision process leading to migration and its implementation. Immigrants offered a variety of reasons leading to their decision to migrate. Although they couched their discourse in terms of economic reality "to make a better living", "to find a good job", closer examination and probing show that social, religious, political, as well as economic factors informed their choice. All these factors prevented the immigrants from achieving their goals in Haiti, from moving from a peripheral position to one closer to the center. *Demele*, as part of the cultural ideas which guide Haitian decision-making processes, spurs them to undertake migration as the only accepted strategy left open to them.

Analysis of the data shows that the immigrants can be divided into two categories - rural and urban - distinguished by the reasons they give for migrating,

their history of prior internal migration, and their
level of education.

Urban Migrants:

One category - the urban - includes migrants who
had already succeeded in crossing some social boundaries, had migrated from a rural to an urban environment in Haiti, and acquired some markers of higher
class status, like command of French, higher education, and a degree of economic stability. These
migrants perceived the Haitian social system as too
rigid, with no opportunity for change, social or
economic mobility. They viewed the political climate
in Haiti as detrimental to social and economic
progress. They felt that class prejudices, discrimination against people of rural and urban poor
origins, against those who do not have the right
entree, or ascribed status, interfered with individual
progress. The following accounts illustrate some of
the features of this category.

Joseph, a 39 year old man, saw no future for himself in Haiti. Because of his position in the class
hierarchy - as a member of the urban Class III - there

was no way for him to fulfill his ambitions. Joseph
said that he did not have the right connections or
patron to help him break away from his ascribed
status, that is, to cross into Class II. Although he
had worked hard at getting an education and acquiring
a skill, he was never able to cross the class boundaries and obtain a footing in the business community.
Out of frustration, he decided to leave Haiti illegally and try his luck elsewhere.

Yves, a 46 year old mason who lived in Port-au-
Prince and left home in search of better economic opportunities, says that the political situation in
Haiti forces Haitians to leave their country. Lack of
work and hunger, he says, are linked to the present
political regime (Duvalier was still in power at the
time of the interview).

Eva grew up in a small town and later moved to
Port-au-Prince with her father and brothers to go to
school. Her mother stayed in the countryside with the
younger children to look after the land. On weekends,
the family would get together in the country. Eva
received her Baccalaureate and also trained as a dental hygienist. She could only earn $15.00/month, be-
cause in Haiti, dental prophylaxis is a luxury few can

afford and dentists seldom hire Hygienists. Instead, she helped her father with his tailoring business. Her husband had to leave Haiti in 1980, for political reasons. She joined him in 1981, leaving a daughter with her mother. She entered the country legally with a tourist visa that has long since expired. A tourist visa, she says, is hard to get and can cost a considerable amount of money. One has to have the proper connections and be ready to pay several individuals along the way to move the papers through the administrative red tape. The process is not always successful and many lose their money.

Barriers remained, and opportunities were denied even to those who tried: Joseph learned a trade, and was a successful entrepreneur, but had no *patron*, no connections in the upper class. Eva learned to speak French, learned a trade and still could not "make it". Migrants, like Joseph, Eva, and Yves, perceive the American social system as more egalitarian - they believe that social and economic mobility are possible for those who *demele ko yo* (work hard), that education is within the reach of everyone, and that language is not an instrument of social cleavage. This image of America is not wrong, it is simply incomplete. It is

the same image shared by all immigrants - the image
that America projects abroad. These Haitian immigrants are socially ambitious individuals who felt
that they had reached a plateau in Haiti (whether social, economic or political), and that migration was
the only alternative left for them. By leaving Haiti,
they were taking a step away from their ascribed
peripheral positions in Haitian social organization.

Once the decision to migrate was taken, the
emigrants had to prepare to leave the country. They
used a variety of networks, such as family and
friends, to find information on transportation, arrange for relatives to look after their interests,
gather the necessary funds and prepare for departure.
Most of them came by sea on small craft (usually sailboats used for fishing) and sometimes on cargo ships;
only a few came by plane. They often talked about
their expectations, and what they envisioned America
to be.

At the time of departure, the majority of individuals in this category had been living in a major
urban center. Some elected to come by plane on a
tourist visa, others had to find passage on *kannte* (A

kannte, also called *bot*, is a small sailboat or-
dinarily used for fishing; a *vape* or *batiman* is a
larger motor craft.[21]).   Either way, their venture
turned out to be costly; ferrying migrants to Florida
and procuring passports and visas is a full-fledged
business in Port-au-Prince. An informant told me that
"individuals traveling on *vape* leaving from Port-au-
Prince and other large towns, like Cap Haitien, Port
de Paix, paid a lot for passage, between $500.00 and
$1,500.00.   People who organized trips from Port-au-
Prince functioned like agencies, businesses.   Those
traveling on *kannte* leaving from Leogane, Petit Goave,
Aux Cayes (smaller towns) paid under $100.00".   But
"*moun an deyo fe bagay patizan, moun pa*" (people from
the countryside do things on their own, they organized
their own groups), they pooled their resources to buy
a boat and food.   Boats did not always keep to their
schedule because of border patrol raids and the
weather, and many who paid in advance lost their
money.

Through a cousin who is a *madam sara* (a woman who
buys goods in Florida or other Caribbean islands to
resell in Haiti), Joseph learned of a man who

recruited people who wished to leave Haiti clandestinely by boat. It took Joseph a while to make up his
mind. He was reluctant to leave under these conditions since he considered himself to be a law-abiding
citizen. When he was ready, his contact introduced
him to the owner of a *batiman* (a motor boat). The
night before he left for Port-de-Paix, where he was to
board the boat, Joseph settled his debts, made a list
of his creditors, and asked his nephew to look after
his interests and his family. The trip cost him
$1240.00. But he expected to be able to earn a lot
more; as he said, "what looks impossible over there
(in Haiti) is nothing here (in America)".

Rural migrants

The second category of Haitian immigrants is composed mostly of individuals of rural origins, who
choose to migrate because of lack of opportunities in
the rural areas and the agricultural sector, land
shortages, low soil productivity, and heavy family
responsibilities. They perceived themselves as being
forced, trapped into migrating by circumstances over
which they have no control. Some had already tried

internal migration, but decided that moving to an urban center in Haiti did not help solve their problems. The cities are crowded, and they did not possess skills that would allow them to earn enough money in an urban milieu. The majority of the people in this group had never been to a major urban center before coming to the United States, had little or no education, were Creole monolingual, and usually practiced *vodou*. A few had been to the Dominican Republic to harvest sugar cane. The following accounts illustrate some of the characteristics of this category of immigrants.

Deslourdes is a 20 year old woman of rural origin; she claims that a *lwa* (vodou spirit) sent her to America. During a *vodou* ceremony in his honor, the spirit spoke to her through her possessed mother, saying: "you better see how you can manage to get to Miami, get a job and send money to feed me". So, every year she sends about $200.00 home to pay for a feast in honor of the spirit.

A 26 year old woman left home to join her husband in Florida. They could not make enough money farming. They have 2 children in Haiti who live with her mother in the family *lakou*.

Marie-Therese left a husband and four children (including a ten month old baby) in their home in the Northern countryside to find a way to help her husband raise their family. She decided to come to Florida with her husband's sister, following the advice of relatives. The women expected to find work easily, earn good money and then return home to start a business.

In this group, the decision to migrate is often seen as being out of the individual's control. Indeed, the process involves the participation of the extended family and sometimes the intervention of supernatural beings. In contrast to the urban category, the rural person emigrates not to fulfill individual goals, but for the good of the extended family. Deslourdes left Haiti after a *lwa* (vodou spirit) commanded her to do so; Lorison's and Marie-Therese's families decided that they had the best chances of succeeding in America. Selection criteria include level of education, skills, as well as more subjective qualifications such as initiative.

Unlike urban migrants who buy passage aboard a *kannte*, migrants from rural areas formed informal *asosyason*; voluntary groups organized along regional and kinship lines. Members of such *asosyason* would *mete ansanm*, pool their resources, to purchase or build a boat and buy provisions. Richman (1985) reports that in some villages the only able men left are either those who have not been successful in getting away, or those who are about to try again.

Lorison, who lived in Ile de la Tortue, a small island off the northern coast, formed an *asosyason* with 12 other people. They got together and contributed between $20.00 and $50.00 each toward the purchase of food and an open sailboat, 15 feet long by 7 feet wide. They left from a deserted area.

Vilnord is a 26 year old fisherman from Ile a Vache, on the southern coast. Since he was the *pilot* of the sailboat which left from Les Cayes, he did not have to contribute toward the purchase of the boat organized by the people from his village. He decided to go to the United States because he had heard good things about that country from those who had left Ile à Vache. "In their letters home they said that it was not hard to find work and they sent money home. I thought that I could do the same and help my parents raise my brothers and sisters". Vilnord's goal is to *demele* and help his kin.

Summary: Push and Pull Factors in Urban and Rural Migration

Cultural ideas of *demele* guide Haitians in their choice to migrate. Migration is one of the culturally accepted strategies to solve problems and to move from periphery to center. Rural Haitians have a long history of seasonal agricultural migration within the Caribbean, as noted in Chapter III. For them, migration has been a traditional way of solving demographic and economic problems.

"Push" factors, in the form of impermeable class boundaries, also force Class III Haitians to leave their country in search of better opportunities. At the same time, there is also a "pull" from America for both categories of migrants, in the form of available work, and a network of kin already in the country who attract the immigrants and assist them in the first stages of immigration. Haitian immigrants hear that "in America there is work for everyone and people mind their own business."

Phase 2. Immigration: _"Mizè nou pase"_ (what we suffered), _"sa nou jwenn"_ (what we found)

"_Nou vin sou batiman bouch louvri. Soley la, nou pran la; lapli a, nou pran la; van, nou pran la. Youn apiye sou lòt._" (We came on an open boat. There we took the sun; there we took the rain; there we took the wind. One leaning on the other).

Immigrants describe their experiences of coming to the United States with ambivalent feelings. They talk about realizing their goal of coming to America. Yet they also describe the hardships of the "crossing", their arrival in the United States and, for most, their bitter experiences in the detention centers.

The immigrants used culturally accepted Haitian strategies to deal with their problems while _"su dlo"_ (on the water), _"lè nou debake"_ (when we landed) in the United States, in the detention camps, and during the initial period of adjustment. One informant managed to fool the system by slipping away unnoticed. Another, a woman, found a way out of her predicament by sheer persistence. When no one was there to receive her the day she was freed, she asked a taxi driver to act as her kin. Immigrants also tapped available networks for help. Relatives and kin (*fanmi*) already in the country are expected to, and do, help others find their way in the United States.

The immigrants' descriptions of the "crossing" are sad memories of hardship and suffering tempered with hopes for a better future. Although in many cases the dreams of freedom and opportunities that sustained them through the ordeal were shattered, there were also happy moments, reunions with relatives and expectations of a better future.

All those who came by boat talk about this experience in great detail. Getting into a sailboat, heading for the unknown, hoping to reach a place three hundred miles away with only the stars as guide, was the ultimate gamble, and the emigrants took all the necessary precautions to ensure a favorable outcome. Christians would carry protective medals, recite prayers, invoke patron saints. Richman (private communication) reports that vodouists carried a variety of sacred objects with them on board the *kannté*, such as empty bottles supposed to contain a potent "air" which they could release when the winds failed, and special amulets given to them by their *lwa*.

Drawings of boats often appear in the migrant camps (on doors, on walls, in pictures that the migrants draw). These boat designs reflect the impact left on the immigrants by this experience. For those who practice *vodou*, the picture of a sailboat is also a very powerful symbol; it is the *veve* (representation, symbol) of *Agwe*, the spirit of the sea. Informants told me that homesick immigrants would draw this *veve* on the ground, then stand on it in the hope that *Agwe* would help them go back home. I noticed that at the beginning of my fieldwork the informants would talk constantly of the crossing and that boats appeared in most of their drawings. As time goes by this experience is being incorporated in the lore of the migration together with other important experiences - to be told, retold, and never forgotten. The crossing is no longer a central topic; it has become assimilated and replaced by other concerns of more immediate relevance. The following accounts illustrate the hardships of the journey to the United States and the unexpected experience of detention camps, as well as the strategies used by the immigrants to cope with these new circumstances.

After losing $510.00 once and getting a discount
on his second try, Jean-Michel, 43 adults and 3
children finally set sail from Mariani, near Port-au-
Prince on August 6, 1981. The trip lasted 12 days.
They spent 3 days in Cuba to mend a broken mast, and
the Cubans fed them. A hurricane blew their ship up
the Gulf of Mexico or the Panama Canal - Jean-Michel
is not sure which. He says that a Canadian ship
rescued them and brought them to Miami - another hour
and they would all have perished. In Miami they were
issued immigration papers and put in the Krome Detention Center. Inmates were allowed to leave as they
found sponsors, and after 10 days, Jean-Michel was
released in the custody of his brother, with whom he
stayed 3 months in Miami. Although he had worked as
an auto mechanic and had a small retail business in
Haiti, he could only find yard work in Florida.

Joseph's *batiman* left Port de Paix with an overload of cargo and emigrants. The passengers were
crowded on the deck without shelter or privacy. Whenever another boat or helicopter would come by,
everyone had to go under deck; they were afraid of the
police. People got sick, hot, thirsty. They carried
6 live goats on board to eat along the way, and they

also cooked beans, plantains and rice. They stopped in Nassau to get water, and six days later arrived in Florida. As they got off the boat in Miami, the passengers were seized by immigration officials. Joseph, a master at *demele*, quickly assessed the situation and decided that he could escape. He called a cab and gave the address of a Haitian family that his cousin had given him. He rented a room there; he had about $230.00. After 3 days he went to the Immigration Office and was issued an I-94. He immediately started attending English classes. After 11 days, he found his first job sewing in a small shop. When it closed he worked as a janitor in a Jewish temple.

Marie-Therese is 26 years old. After her husband left Haiti in 1980, she did not receive news from him. Then she heard that a few people from her village planned to leave on a small boat. She contributed $10.00, they *mete ansanm*, pooled their resources, and bought corn. They had a difficult crossing. She says that they spent 22 days "*su dlo*", on the water, and a few days in Cuba to fix the boat. They stopped in several places to get fresh water and food. At times they drank sea water, and it made them sick.

> While I was on the water, she says, he
> (the husband) sent me a little money in
> Haiti. Then they sent news to him that

I was on the water. When my family told
him I was on the water he was surprised.
I had a friend who lived nearby, she
called her brother (in Miami) on the
phone to tell him she was going on the
same boat as me, and to tell my husband.
When the boat landed in Florida,
everyone was taken into jail (Krome
detention Center). My husband came to
the camp, he gave my name, they called
me, so he found me. He brought me
clothes and things. They did not let me
go. He came back to see me and bring me
things and they did not let me go. When
the day came for me to be released,
nobody came to pick me up; they did not
know that I was going to be freed. But
I had a plan and I went to my cousin in
Miami. I ran away because they said
that those who did not have anybody to
pick them up were going to be sent back
to camp. When I heard that, I got off
the bus quickly, found a taxi; I had all
my papers with me. I had some money
that my husband had brought and my
cousin's address. But the taxi driver
did not accept any money, he just
brought me to my cousin's.

Marie-Therese then went to join her husband who lived
in Fort Pierce where he was picking grapefruit. Since
her arrival she has been sick and unable to work and
send money home. At the time of the interview, she
had been in the States for two years. She had had a
miscarriage, a difficult pregnancy which ended in a
Cesarean, and was again experiencing another difficult
pregnancy.

Marc arrived in Florida in 1980; he and several
friends got together and bought a boat and food. They

left from Leogane (near Port-au-Prince). They spent
sixteen days in Cuba,

> they were very good to us, we played
> soccer, they fed us. But they did not
> let us roam alone for fear that we might
> get hurt. There are lots of arms around
> there! They gave us housing, took us
> sightseeing. They wanted us to stay.

But they left aboard another ship. There were 29
people on board, 9 women and 20 men.

> Then we got lost and were headed for
> Havana when a boat told us that it was
> not Miami. They gave us food and water.
> Six days later we landed in Miami Beach.
> The police came. They gave us clean
> clothes, put us on a bus that took us to
> a hospital to get shots. We spent a few
> days in a camp, then we went to a hotel.
> A pastor came to get us, we spent four
> days with him. Then a guy named Norman
> came to recruit workers for a white man.
> We went to work in a factory, a plywood
> factory. We were well looked after.

Only desperation, determination, and a strong
belief that a better life is possible in the U.S.
could prompt the immigrants to leave home, family, and
face the unknown in such a manner. Innocent said :
"*Lè nou kite Ayiti, nou konn nap viv pi alèz. Icit
malere viv pi fasil*" (When we left Haiti, we knew that
we would live more comfortably. Here [in the U.S.]
poor people live better). The vision of life in
America, accompanied by the Haitian concept of *demele*
and an obstinate faith that in the end there will be a

solution, a way out of the predicament, sustained them. *"Bondye bon"* (God is good) Haitians say. *"Bondye bon"* is a saying that Haitians often use when talking about their problems or explaining a particular predicament. It implies complete trust that if one tries hard, in the end, good will prevail and everything will be fine. Although in most cases their initial experiences were negative, the immigrants still believe that life in America is better than life in Haiti. They hoped to blend in, disappear from the public eye and go on with their lives.

When intercepted by the American authorities, Haitian immigrants were interned in detention centers such as Krome, Florida; Ray Brook, New York; and Fort Allen in Puerto Rico. Most Haitians describe their incarceration as their worst experience. After successfully completing their perilous journey, starting their new life in a detention camp was a difficult experience.

Immigrants expressed anger at being locked up. Underlying their anger was hopelessness; they felt that they were no longer in control. While they had risked their lives to enter the United States, in the detention camps they felt powerless, at the mercy of

others.] The purpose of their exodus had been taken
away, they could only *chita*, wait and see. They survived, sustained by cultural survival mechanisms embodied in the concept of *demele*. Some escaped, others
revolted, and a few accepted the option of going back
home.

Linor arrived in Florida in September, 1981. He
spent two and a half months at the Krome Detention
Center in Florida and nine months in Fort Allen,
Puerto Rico. He talks of his Krome experience in unfavorable terms: "When I arrived here, they put me in
jail, they made me eat without washing my mouth, they
made me go to bed without washing my body". He felt
mistreated, dehumanized, powerless. After being
released from Fort Allen, he bought himself a ticket
for New York City where he had relatives. He was
greatly disappointed and his dreams of freedom were
shattered. Gesner tried to escape several times from
Krome, but every time the police brought him back.
Finally "my brother came and signed me out".

Frenel came to America in 1981.

> When I arrived, the Immigration people
> put me in a camp. I spent six months in
> the Krome Center. At that time there
> were a lot of Haitians and Americans who
> came to demonstrate. When I saw that I
> was not about to be released, I should
> have escaped. I spent five days on a

hunger strike. They brought food, but
even if I had wanted to eat, the 'gro
neg' (bullies, strong men) in the camp
would have beaten me up. They said we
had to go on a hunger strike. I got
tired, fed up. So, one day I climbed
the fence, jumped and ran. So now I
don't have any (legal) papers.

Some who escaped incarceration had a different
problem. They were free, but they did not have legal
documents, could not find work, and lived in fear of
being apprehended.

Hubert has been in the U.S. since 1977. He came
by boat and had no legal papers. He said that "life
used to be harder for illegal aliens, people could be
easily deported". He had to live clandestinely and
moved often; he was afraid of being caught by the INS.
He stayed with different relatives, did odd jobs for
which he could only be paid in cash since he had "no
papers, no social security". In 1981, he presented
himself to the Immigration officials with the new boat
people, and was granted an I-94 and a social security
card. Now he can work legally and stop hiding.

When they were sou d'lo (on the water, i.e. at
sea) and while in detention camps, the immigrants were
at the mercy of the elements and of others. There
were few opportunities to use demele strategies other
than those that dealt with immediate survival. They

were all in the same boat, so to speak, rural and urban, peasants seeking a way to help their kin, and socially ambitious urban individuals striving for social
as well as economic advancement, *eseye pouse pi lwen*
(trying to go forward). As they arrived in Southern
Florida or were let out of detention, they tried to
re-establish the traditional rural-urban distinction
and hierarchy that characterized Haitian society.

Phase 3. Resettlement: *Peyi icit* (this country)

Once in the U.S., the immigrants had to come to
terms with reality, and for some it was a rude awaken-
ing. What they had dreamed of when they left home did
not always coincide with what they found. One informant told me that he had envisioned Miami to be a very
large modern city with no trees and greenery. He was
surprised to find slums, weeds, roaches, and rodents.
Several immigrants had no clear understanding of
American geography; many equated Miami and Florida,
New York City and New York State. A woman said that
she came thinking that she would have the choice between working as a servant, or as a cleaning woman in
a hotel or a restaurant. She believed that jobs would

be plentiful and well paid; she had given no thought to qualifications or language barriers.

After the immigrants had accomplished their short term goal of entering the United States, braving great odds and legal difficulties, they were faced with the problem of finding a place for themselves in this new environment. Most rural immigrants had never been in a large urban center in Haiti, and were awed by the complexities of life in America. They relied on relatives, friends, or individuals from their own villages and towns who were already in the States for help and advice. Communication networks between Haiti and America and within the Haitian immigrant communities in the United States relay messages and disseminate information. Telephone communications, correspondence, cassette recordings and the *telediol* (word of mouth, literally broadcast by mouth) keep individuals abreast of what is happening at home and in the various immigrant communities. The communities are always abuzz with all sorts of rumors, misinterpreted news items, information regarding job opportunities, and population movements. These networks are crucial for the new immigrants, urban as well as rural. They provide them with a variety of information regarding

housing, the whereabouts of acquaintances, and individuals and organizations which can help with the
resettlement process. Even though the networks
relayed news of drownings, interceptions, and incarceration to the people in Haiti, more immigrants came.
They either believed that they could endure these
"minor disturbances" and go on with their lives, or
that it would not happen to them.

The first priority of a new arrival from either
social category is to find a place to stay.
Patron/client relationships developed between the immigrants and those who took them in, whether relatives
or friends. The latter would be *reskonsab*, responsible for the socialization of the immigrant to the
new environment; in return the new immigrant would
perform services and contribute to the household expenses. Sometimes people would compete for new arrivals and I was never sure, from what my informants
said, whether the patrons only derived economic gains
or also prestige from these relationships. The following account illustrates the dynamics of
patron/client relationships.

After Lorison, a rural migrant, was released from
Krome, he went to live with a cousin. She bought him

clothes, introduced him around and gave him money until he found a job. Lorison says that he did not *rete
avèk* (live with) his cousin, but that she was
"reskonsab" (responsible) for him.   The distinction
here is very subtle. *Rete avèk* would imply a sexual
arrangement between Lorison and his cousin.   The position of *reskonsab* carried rights,   duties   and
privileges   for   both   parties: the   cousin   was
"responsible" for him legally and supported him until
he could find a job; she introduced him to people who
could help him, and socialized him to the rules of his
new community.   In return, he paid room and board and
gave "her money when she needed something".   Their
patron/client relationship does not violate Haitian
cultural ideas regarding gender relations.   Males and
females do not stand in a fixed hierarchical relationship toward each other.   In certain cases women become
head of a *lakou*, and they also play key roles in *vodou*
rituals.

A year after his arrival, Lorison met his brother
and chose to go live with him.   Although Lorison was
vague about his part of the bargain, it is clear that
he parted in unfriendly terms with his cousin, as if
he had broken an agreement.

In some cases the immigrants entered other types
of relationships, such as those of kinship amity
shared by all members of an extended family. Salomon
is a member of a large rural extended family. Several
of his kin had already migrated. Some, including his
mother's brothers, were living in Miami. His uncles
paid for his trip on a *kannte*. When he arrived in
Florida, he went to live in Fort Pierce with his
brother-in-law until he found a job and a place of his
own. He remained in close touch with all his relatives and contacted them whenever he had problems and
needed advice. His case demonstrates that kinship
ties and obligations extend outside of the confines of
the *lakou*, and of Haiti.

Thus, the process of adaptation in the United
States is not done haphazardly; there are structures
already in place in the United States that absorb the
immigrants. At the beginning the immigrants have a
limited choice of alternatives. They are channeled to
different systems according to various factors:
origins, network affiliations, skills. Although their
initial expectations are idealized, Haitians are
realistic and soon understand that barriers exist that
they cannot yet cross. As they resettle in America,

immigrants re-establish the familiar rural-urban oppositions that characterize Haitian social structure.
People of urban origins tend to choose urban centers,
and those with a rural background gravitate toward
small agricultural communities. Although practical
considerations and personal aspirations influence
their decisions, their choice of residence is to some
extent also a way of asserting their Haitian identities. Immigrants usually go to places where they
have friends and relatives, as well as to areas where
they feel comfortable, can blend in, and go unnoticed.

NEW SETTLEMENTS: URBAN AND RURAL

In Florida boat people settled in two types of
communities; rural agricultural communities, and ethnic neighborhoods in urban centers. By far the
largest concentration of Haitians in Florida is in
Little Haiti, one of Miami's oldest neighborhoods. A
1982 survey estimated that about 25,000 Haitians lived
in Little Haiti (Stepick 1984).

Little Haiti is a vibrant and rapidly expanding
economic community. Most of its businesses are
family-owned and consist of small retail and service

operations that cater to the special needs of the residents. Unemployment is high, and few people have full-time, steady jobs. Most survive by doing seasonal, part-time, and temporary work outside of the neighborhood. Few accept public assistance, and only 25% receive food stamps (HACAD 1984). *Komès*, (small scale retail), a typical Haitian occupation among women, is also a way of earning a living here. Several open air markets, like those organized in Haiti, flourish in Little Haiti (Stepick 1984, 1984b).

Demographic surveys reveal a fast-growing, predominantly male population of working age - 53.0% of the population is male and the mean age is 24.3 years. In 1983, 30% of all the Haitian households in the neighborhood reported a pregnancy, and the average household size was 3.9 persons. Immigrants live together in order to share housing costs and recreate familiar extended family units. Men and women form consensual unions in the United States, and in most cases, both have conjugal partners and offspring in Haiti. Both also have strong family commitments in Haiti in addition to their local familial responsibilities. For all, the adjustment to American life

is a stressful process. The immigrants are torn between personal aspirations and expectations, the
economic and social realities of their present situation, and conflicts over their cultural identities
(HACAD 1983).

Inhabitants of Little Haiti maintain a low profile
and remain socially isolated. They have experienced
prejudice and discrimination. The negative publicity
they received over the tuberculosis and AIDS epidemics
has created further barriers between them and the
other ethnic groups, inside and outside the community.
At the same time, Haitians are eager to participate in
programs that will increase their skills and employment prospects (Nachman 1983, 1984, 1984b).

Haitian boat people also settled in several
agricultural communities in Southern Florida's Dade
and Boward counties along the Western shores, around
Orlando and Tampa. These communities are also inhabited by other agricultural workers, such as Black
Americans and other people of Caribbean origins.
There is little in the literature about them. The
data collected during my own fieldwork present the
following demographic composition and social organization which may well characterize these communities.

The population is dominated by young males and the level of education among these immigrants is lower than that of urban dwellers. There are three times more males among the rural immigrant population, and the population averages two years of formal education. There seems to be less emphasis on participation in job training and other educational programs among them than among the urban population. It appears that in communities like Immokale, Belle Glade, Fort Pierce, Vero Beach, Winter Haven, and Lake Wales, which are located in agricultural areas, most Haitian immigrants are employed in the agricultural sector. Most of the immigrants I have talked with say that there is sufficient work in the farms at harvest time, but that there is little else to do after the harvest or outside the agricultural sector. Nachman (1984) also points out that Haitians in Boward County are better off financially, and have access to better living conditions, health facilities, and social service programs than residents of Little Haiti.

Migrant farm workers, as well as some of the Haitian immigrants living in Rochester, came from these rural communities in Florida. My data indicate that most migrant farm workers go back to the rural agricultural settlements at the end of the harvest season. Most of the Rochester residents had spent some time in Little Haiti before settling in the city, while others had lived in agricultural communities.

The Florida Haitian communities are homogeneous, young communities of people of urban poor and rural origins, and they remain socially isolated from the rest of American society. There is little interaction within the communities between Haitians and the other residents. The Florida communities, especially the farm communities, are Haitian enclaves where change happens slowly. They are reminiscent of the Haitian immigrant communities of Cuba, the Dominican Republic and Bahamas described in Chapter III. They re-create to some extent the atmosphere of Haitian small towns and rural areas.

However, isolation is also a strategy to fend off some of the dangers and difficulties that the larger society presents. One of the most threatening - the uncertainty of their legal status - looms large over the fate of Haitian boat people in the United States. This uncertainty, and the fear of deportation, stand in the way of their assimilation into American society and are important factors in the development of "isolationist" strategies.

Travay kontra (contract work, i.e. migrant farm labor)

Pressed into finding new sources of employment, chèche yon jan pou demele tèt nou (trying to find a solution to our problems), Haitian immigrants living in Florida were easily attracted to migrant farm labor. This niche seemed to meet the need of Haitian boat people to maintain a low degree of visibility, to find an occupation that required little skill and to earn some money. Recruitment into this line of work, or the "migrant stream," was done mainly through informal networks within the Haitian community. Crew bosses relying on Haitian interpreters and former workers organize their crews in Florida in the spring and then take them north. The crews stop in several places along the Eastern stream to harvest crops. They arrive in Wyoming County in early September in time to pick potatoes. This process of recruitment into the farm labor system is illustrated in the following accounts.

After trying several odd jobs in Florida, Joseph contracted to work as a migrant worker through a Haitian friend from Palmetto, Florida. He worked in the packing house of a potato farm near Castile, New York. He worked long and hard hours, but found that he could save money with the food stamps that the workers are given.

When his gardening job in Miami ended, Jean-Robert "made" a contract with a crew boss. A *kontra*, he says, is a verbal agreement between a *blan* (white man, foreigner, usually used to refer to the crew leader), and a worker. The crew boss had Haitian interpreters who helped him contact available workers. They first went to Virginia, then came to Castile, New York, to pick potatoes and then tomatoes.

Gertrude lived in Fort Pierce and has worked as a farm hand since she came from Haiti. She has been a migrant farm worker before. The previous year she was in Pennsylvania, and the year before (1981), she worked near Buffalo, New York. She always works with Haitians. This (1983) was her first year in Wyoming County and her first experience picking potatoes. In Florida, Gertrude picks oranges and tomatoes. She was here with her younger sister Yolette. The workers, they say, were contacted by the crew leader who took them here on two big buses. They could not remember when they had left Fort Pierce or how long they had been gone. While on the road they would stop often to repair the busses and sleep.

When Marie-Therese joined her husband in Fort Pierce, he was working as a farm hand picking flowers and grapefruit. This (1983) was his second migrant season and her first.

Migrant labor, *travay kontra*, was seen as a better alternative than unemployment. It was a form of *demele* that suited the immigrants' lifestyle, their background, and their needs.

The immigrants perceived that leaving Haiti and coming to the United States was a move from periphery to center, or, in their own words, to *pouse pi lwen* (to push further). Migration was a culturally accepted form of *demele* and an alternate way to "make it". Once in the United States, however, they had to re-adjust their strategies. Again *demele*, family obligations, and the desire to achieve personal goals pushed them to find other solutions.

So far this study has investigated the historical, social, cultural, economic, and political components

of Haitian migration of rural and urban poor populations. Migration has been described as a culturally
accepted strategy to move from periphery to center.
Causes for migration have been analyzed in terms of
how Haitians themselves talk about it, and in terms of
the Haitian concept of *demele* (to come up with a solution, to get out of a bind). The latest wave of illegal immigration of Haitians into the United States
was the focus of this chapter. Adaptation was used as
an analytical concept to investigate the ways in which
Haitian immigrants, specifically boat people, learn to
function in a different and new culture and society.
It has been suggested that the cultural ideas that
Haitians have, their goals and expectations, their
perception of American society, as well as reality in
the United States, shape and limit their adaptation to
this new environment. The following chapter examines
immigrants who chose the migrant labor system in order
to create a better life, as they perceive it, for
themselves and their kin.

CHAPTER V

MIGRANT LABOR
A WAY TO *"POUSE PI LWEN"*, TO GO FURTHER

This chapter concentrates on migrant labor as one of the options open to Haitian immigrants. The options available to Haitian immigrants are limited by their lack of marketable skills and education, as well as poor command of the English language. In addition, the immigrants face barriers imposed by the host society, such as uncertain legal status and the American class structure. The following sections offer an overview of migrant life, the social place that Haitian workers create for themselves in that milieu, and the adjustments they make in order to function in it. In this new environment, roles are re-defined to fit the new circumstances in terms of old cultural values. The function of *demele* is always present as the immigrants try to make the best of their uncertain situation. Some view farm labor as a transient occupation, as something to do to help make ends meet while waiting for a permanent job. Others perceive it as a transitory step in their adaptation to American society, as one occupation that may lead to something better.

MIGRANT CAMPS

Migrant camps are bleak, isolated, and in-
hospitable places. In the camps that I visited,
Haitian as well as mixed camps, only the bare neces-
sities are provided and no attention is given to comfort or aesthetic elements. Most camps are either
trailers, old farm houses, or low, cinder block structures, consisting of several small rooms opening
directly to the outside. They are reminiscent of
cheap motels. Each room houses a family unit, or two
or three single adults. In some camps, single men are
housed in communal rooms called "bull pens". There is
a common kitchen, an all-purpose room where people
eat, talk, play games, or fight. Hygienic facilities
are often sub-standard, but usually consist of
separate showers and toilets for men and women.

The poor physical conditions and barren surroundings of migrant camps project a desolate and depress-
ing image. Gas stoves have leaks, old machinery and
garbage dumpsters are scattered around, screen doors
bang in the wind, laundry is hung to dry on bushes or
barbed wire fences, and mud puddles or barren, rocky
grounds accost the visitor. There is a total lack of

privacy; walls are thin, and rooms are overcrowded. Inside, the units reflect the individual character of their tenants. Some attempt to decorate the bare walls with pictures torn from magazines and newspapers. Pieces of fabric are hung on windows as curtains. Sheets or blankets make room dividers between parents' and children's beds, or between each adult sleeping area. Some rooms are neat and cozy, others are messy and cluttered. Potato dust permeates everything.

Camps are often isolated, tucked away in the middle of potato fields, or barely visible from the road. They are usually located far from towns, shopping areas, or recreational facilities. Transportation is a persistent problem. Moreover, the migrants are often uneasy in these places and the shopkeepers are suspicious of the migrants. Therefore, relations between the host communities and the migrant workers are tense and uneasy, neither knowing much about the other (Yamashita 1984). With no access to outside means of recreation, the camp becomes for the migrant a "self-contained universe," and one with limited social space available to each individual. Isolation, fatigue, and overcrowding generate tension, social conflicts, and anxieties, as well as apathy, anger, and boredom. It is not surprising, therefore, that alcoholism and gambling are major problems, that inter-personal conflicts arise, and that arguments, fights, and physical violence are ways of settling differences.

Yet camps are also places where human values and dignity are ever-present. In this transient atmosphere everything happens fast, relationships develop rapidly and differences are quickly, if not always peacefully, resolved. Great value is placed on sharing and helping others. Workers are receptive to outside interest and eager to talk about themselves. Individuality is important to a migrant worker, and it is reflected in the way people dress, talk, and organize their social space. Those who are talented decorate the walls; others sing; and many like to draw and participate in storytelling and music-making sessions. Creative art forms are outlets that the workers use to express their feelings about the migrant labor system, about their work, and about their place in the larger social system.

Each camp has a special character that is partially dependent upon its ethnic composition. Other factors, such as the physical layout of the camp, and the demographic composition of its population also affect its social organization. While doing fieldwork, I became interested in the dynamics of camp life. I noted the mechanisms used to maintain equilibrium between different factions, the elements that defined the lines of cleavages between the factions, and how people dealt with cultural and social changes, expectations, and loneliness. I will describe two camps, Lake Road Camp, an all-Haitian camp located in a motel-like structure, and a mixed camp, composed of several trailers and an old farmhouse, which will be referred to as Jo's Camp. Each camp highlights Haitian categories of opposition - such as rural-urban, lack of education-education, powerlessness-power, black-white - that reemerge in the United States.

Lake Road Camp

Lake Road Camp sits on top of a hill, along a dirt road, surrounded by potato fields. Fall evenings can be beautiful and under the clear sky the camp looks deceptively quiet. Seventeen rooms housed thirty

adults and three children. Each family unit occupied
one room.   Seven young adult males lived in a large
bull pen. Four older men shared two rooms, and an
older woman had a room to herself. During the week,
by seven a.m., the camp looked deserted: the children
have left for the day care center and school, and the
adults have gone to work. On rainy days the adults
remained in camp. The women washed clothes by hand,
and cleaned their rooms. The men engaged in various
chores, such as fixing cars. When they were not working, the adults would sit in the common room playing
cards, talking, cooking, or just relaxing. In the
evenings, after work, people showered in the two back
rooms. On warm evenings, men would use a hose outside, and mothers bathed their children in laundry
tubs. While individuals took great care of their personal grooming and living quarters, the common areas
were always in a chaotic state. Potato dust permeated
the whole camp, and field flies were everywhere.
Music from cassette players could be heard at all
times.

Except for one couple who had been married in
Haiti, most family units were formed in the United

States, some in the camps that very season. Common-
law unions, or *plasaj*, which are very common in Haiti
among rural and urban poor populations, also emerge in
the camps. Other forms of Haitian households also appear. One family unit consisted of a man, his six
year-old daughter, his fifteen year-old nephew, and
his older brother.

Lake Road Camp was not efficiently run. Relations
between Onell, the crew leader, and his crew were
strained. All the workers in Lake Road Camp had been
recruited in Fort Pierce, Florida. Some had worked
together during other seasons. The crew arrived the
first of September. By the seventeenth, five adults
and their two children had returned to Florida. Some
claimed that Onell was inept as a crew leader and had
promised more than he could deliver. Others wanted to
give him a chance. On the 24th, after a terrible argument with Onell, nine more adults left to go pick
apples in Wayne County. By October first, only nine
adults and one child remained. One of the men who had
left to work elsewhere returned. The remaining group
settled into a routine, and room assignments were
changed. Two Black Americans stayed for a few days,
then left. The camp closed down on October 22nd, as

work ended. Five adults were moved to a larger camp to await transportation. Onell and the others left in their cars. By the end of the season it was evident that the crew leader had not been able to keep his crew together, to provide enough work for them, and to take charge of running the camp efficiently.

In their spare time, the workers played cards (pokino or poker for money) or dominoes, sang, drummed, and talked. Their conversations covered a wide range of topics and would often end in heated arguments, particularly those dealing with religion. Sometimes the workers would draw, write letters, or tape messages to be sent home.

The people of Lake Road Camp were farmers in Haiti and do not have transferable skills, enough education or enough English to enable them to obtain better paying jobs. For them, migrant labor in the summer and fall, and contract farm work in the winter, will be the way of life. Like other immigrants, they place their hope for a better future with the next generation. They wait and see, while clutching to *demele*.

Jo's Camp

Jo's Camp is one of two large camps owned by a grower. It consists of several trailers, neatly arranged on the hillside, and an old farm house. In order to visit the camp, one is issued a permit from the grower and the Camp Committee, following an interview. The visitor is required to comply with a set of rules designed to "prevent the introduction of various agricultural pests, foster the privacy and rights of association of farm residents and maintain the farm economy" (1984 Rules for access to Murdock's Farms and Labor Camps). The applicant must sign "under penalty of perjury" a form in which he/she promises that " at no time will I or anyone under my direction ...interfere in any way with any contract existing between Murdock, his Crew Leader, or the Crew Leader and his workers". Mr. Murdock's camps are far from being luxurious, but they are well-maintained. He has been doing business with the same crew leaders for several years. He knows the workers and takes an active part in the harvest. Nevertheless, he still pays .25c/ 75lb bag of potatoes, and is quick to penalize the workers. Although he gives bonuses and treats the

workers to a barbecue dinner at the end of the season,
it is rumored that he withholds .1c/bag throughout the
season for that purpose.

Jo's Camp had a mixed population. There were
Haitians, Black Americans, and a few other people of
Caribbean origin. Several Haitians and two Black
Americans occupied the farmhouse. Each trailer could
hold six to seven adults. I did not see any children
in Jo's Camp, and there were more men than women. The
farmhouse was centrally located and more spacious.
Evening classes and clinics were held there. I
usually met people and conducted my interviews in the
farmhouse, but I visited several informants in their
trailers as well. The chaos and untidiness of Lake
Road Camp was absent here. The trailers that I
visited and the farmhouse were clean and tidy. I
speculate that the co-residential groups and units
being smaller, the tenants could have considered the
common areas to be more like an extension of their
private space. Moreover, the Haitians I saw there
came from Palmetto, and Little Haiti in Florida. They
were more educated, more sophisticated and perhaps
more able to negotiate better contract terms than the
people in Lake Road. Haitians in Jo's Camp had also

been urban dwellers in Haiti, and possessed a variety of skills. There was a tailor, an artisan, a mason, a cobbler. The majority of Haitian workers could read and write and were eager to learn English.

Demographic differences between Lake Road and Jo's Camps indicate that Haitian settlements in Florida follow patterns that closely duplicate the distribution of social categories present in Haitian society. As already mentioned in Chapter IV, Fort Pierce is a more rural environment than Palmetto, and Little Haiti is an urban settlement.

No one left Jo's Camp during the season. Two of the Haitians who had expressed the wish to remain in Rochester decided against leaving at the last minute. I estimate that there were close to one hundred workers in Jo's Camp, at least one-third of them Haitians. As the crew was so large, the workers were divided into groups headed by assistant crew leaders. One such leader was a young Haitian man named Henri. He was dynamic, efficient, and well-organized. He had been coming up with the same crew for several years and enjoyed the work. He was in charge of several Haitians and the two Black Americans who lived in the

farm house. His job required a good deal of organization and mediation between crew leader and workers.
He could read and write in French, speak "enough
English to get by and can write it a little". He kept
a log with the names of his workers, the amounts they
earned, filled worker compensation and insurance
claims, etc. The atmosphere was not as tense as in
Lake Road Camp, although some problems did arise. The
workers seemed to accept Henri's leadership even
though he was younger than most.

There were only male workers in the farmhouse.
They shared cooking and cleaning duties. The kitchen
was always clean. There were dishes in the cupboard
and a stove that was in good repair. The Haitians
stated that the Black Americans living with them were
clean, neat, did not drink, and that "they associated
with them." Since the camp's population was scattered
among the farmhouse and the trailers, Jo's Camp lacked
the feeling of unity that characterized Lake Road
Camp. The mood was one of determination, to make the
best of a bad situation, which sometimes bordered on
frustration and despair. In Florida, the workers in
Jo's Camp were either unemployed or did part-time

menial tasks. They looked at farm work as a com-
promise, a way to make good money while waiting for
something better.

As in Lake Road Camp, the workers spent several
evenings during the season discussing the legalization
of their immigration status, happenings in the Haitian
community, and news from home. Following Haitian
migration patterns, several of them had been to other
places prior to coming to the United States. These
included Nassau, the Dominican Republic, and French
Guyana. They had already tried several avenues to
move from periphery to center. Most Haitians in Jo's
Camp had been urban dwellers in Haiti, and were at
least one generation removed from peasantry and *vodou*.
Several informants were fervent Christians, mainly
Protestants, who took their faith seriously. Although
I did not find any who admitted to practicing *vodou*,
most still believed in the powers of spirits. According to Haitians, Christianity is a more powerful faith
than *vodou*. It protects one against the agency of
malevolent beings.

Contrary to the chaos of Lake Road, I never witnesses any brawls or loud arguments in Jo's Camp.
People made political jokes about the ineptitude of

the Haitian government, its policies, about "Reagan" -
who personifies the American Government to them, and
about the stupidity of Haitians. The satire was often
brutal and well-appreciated. A joke I heard one evening reflected the pervasiveness of political repression in Haiti. A woman's son named Duvalier fell off
a tree. She was upset and went around screaming,
pulling her hair. When people in the *lakou* asked why
she was so distressed, she answered: *"Duvalier monte
sou pye mango a, lè fini Duvalier..."* (Duvalier
climbed the mango tree then he..) and she slapped her
hand on the ground. She had to mimic the action of
falling since it would have been politically dangerous
to associate the word *tombe* (fell) with the
President's name. Through the medium of jokes, the
workers seemed to vent their emotional frustrations,
work out conflicts, and make commentaries on socially
sensitive topics.

Several factors contributed to the difference of
atmosphere in both camps: the leadership, the physical
layout of the camps, the demographic and social composition of their respective populations, and the
aspirations of the workers. For some of those without
marketable skills and education, migrant labor was to

remain a way of life. For those who had a trade and some education, it was only a temporary job. They would eventually find work outside the stream, or move to more profitable and steady occupations.

An interesting theme that emerged during my fieldwork concerned the relationship between the quality of leadership and conflict resolution in the camps. In Lake Road Camp for example, no one wanted to take on the responsibility of arranging for the care of the common areas. As crew leader, Onell should have had the authority to do so, but he lacked the attributes of leadership. The workers often complained that Onell was ineffective as a crew leader; he was unable to negotiate with the *bòs man* for good fields for his pickers. They said that a good crew leader would make sure that his crew would at least get a mixture of good and bad plots - Onell's crew was always assigned to pick rocky fields. During a growers' meeting in September of 1984, a grower complained about one of his crews from the Lake Road Camp. According to him, the workers were stuffing rocks in the bags; they also grabbed more than their share of bags. They would decide not to work after getting to the fields, and still expect to be paid.

When I asked Onell about this, he said that the
workers were not happy with the job, that they did not
want to work. The workers laughed at the complaints;
one said, "how could I put rocks in the bags? I already can't lift a bag of potatoes, how could I carry
rocks?".

Onell lacked the experience, knowledge, and social
status necessary to run a crew. The workers sensed
his weakness, and the egalitarianism so characteristic
of rural Haitians surfaced. The workers would not
take orders from someone they regarded as inept. In
their eyes, Onell was not a *bòs*. It is also important
to note here that this particular crew consisted of
rural Haitians with very little or no education. Most
of them had been farmers in Haiti. They were accustomed to working alone or in *kombit* teams (corvee) at
special times: to clean a new field, dig irrigation
channels, etc. Therefore, they were not receptive to
new work techniques, and it would have taken someone
of higher social status or more experience to teach
them the techniques required in potato harvesting.

On the other hand, Henri, the assistant crew
leader in Jo's Camp, ran a tight crew. The workers
accepted his leadership, even though he was younger

than most of them. Henri was an educated man, spoke
English, and the workers trusted him. He was able to
explain and teach them the work techniques in terms
that they understood. He could safeguard their interests, and relate their problems to the grower. There
were no major work related problems in Jo's Camp.

MIGRANT WORKERS IN WYOMING COUNTY, NEW YORK

Potatoes are the most common crop in Wyoming
County, the area in which fieldwork was conducted.
Potato harvesting is usually considered low status
work. It is stoop labor that requires minimal skill,
and it is the lowest-paying of farm occupations. The
mechanical harvest of potatoes used to be a costly and
inefficient operation because of the hilly and rocky
terrain of this region. Recently, however, growers
have been taking advantage of technological innova-
tions and large farms are being mechanized in increasing numbers. This development results in decreased
hiring of farmhands, and is changing the pattern of
seasonal migration in the northeast. The number of
migrants in the Genesee Valley has decreased steadily.
It has gone down from 2,400 in 1971, at the peak of

the season, to around 1,100 in 1982 (Mattera and Watson 1983:4).

The migrant stream is also experiencing demographic changes. In the forties, Southern Black American families were the major source of seasonal labor.

> Those early workers, most of whom travelled in family groups and were themselves former farmers, began dropping out from the stream (for economic reasons), being replaced increasingly by the sweepings of barrooms and skid rows. Arguably, the quality of the work force declined, more incentive was given to mechanization (Mattera and Watson 1983: 6).

The introduction of Haitian immigrants into the migrant stream has been interesting to observe. Mattera and Watson (1983) looked at alcohol use among potato pickers in Livingston and Wyoming counties, New York. They found that alcohol consumption was high among older, unattached Black American workers. They also note that "those Haitians who had been in the migrant stream two years were adopting the drinking habits of the migrants" (p.45). Yamashita studied Haitian apple and cherry pickers in Wayne County, New York. She found that "communication among the Haitians and other migrant groups and with employers is limited," that fluency in English was a problem and that "most Haitians aspired to advance to other types of work. Most do not find farmwork satisfactory" (1984:8).

Haitians are considered good workers, eager to learn, and to take advantage of educational oppor- tunities. At the peak of the 1980 season, there were 21 migrant camps in the potato farming region, and ap- proximately 600 workers - none of them Haitian. By 1982, there were only ten camps, and no more than 450 workers - perhaps half of them Haitians - at the peak of the season (Mattera and Watson 1983).

It appears that Haitian boat people have created a niche for themselves in this environment. The follow- ing section examines the ways in which Haitian im- migrants "make it" in the migrant stream, how they react to migrancy (*travay kontra*), and what strategies they use in the process of their adaptation to the United States.

MAKING IT IN THE MIGRANT STREAM: *DEMELE TÈT NOU* (FINDING A WAY OUT)

This section traces the strategies that Haitian immigrants use to "make it" in a unique milieu, the

American migrant labor system.   The migrant stream
represents a special type of American setting, with a
distinctive character and organization.   For the
Haitian boat people, migrant farm work is a form of
demele, a strategic choice.   What Haitian immigrants
say about their experience, as well as the way they
structure their lives as migrant farm workers, shed
light on the extent to which Haitian traditional
beliefs, practices, and social organization influence
the adaptation process.   The migrant labor system is
an established structure, and Haitian immigrants who
enter the stream bring with them a unique way of solving problems, organizing labor, resolving conflicts,
etc.   These two systems, Haitian and American, engage
in an interplay in which both are transformed.   The
migrant labor system (and in a wider sense American
society), and the Haitian immigrants (and in a wider
sense Haitian society), affect one another.   The
migrant labor system adjusts to the values and organization of the people who enter it, and the Haitian
immigrants are influenced by the demands and structure
of the migrant stream.   Thus, Haitian strategies for
making it reflect elements of both systems.   The
milieu in which adaptation takes place is American,

but it is interpreted and given meaning in term of Haitian culture and values.

In the following section, the informants' statements on a variety of topics, such as working conditions, religion, and family organization, are presented and analyzed. The analysis takes into consideration already described elements, such as social, cultural, economic, historical, and political factors. It stresses the importance of these factors and of the structure of the receiving community in tracing strategies for "making it". It demonstrates how *demele* motivates the immigrants, infuses meaning in their action, and how Haitian ideas on social hierarchy affect their adaptation to the United States.

Working conditions: "*m redi kòm otan m kapab*", (I stretch my body to its limits)

All migrants had mixed feelings about farm work, particularly potato picking. Even those who had prior experience in working the land found potato harvesting strenuous. They accepted the living and working conditions as a necessary evil, but were more concerned about the pay. They indicated that they were here to *demele tèt nou* (for us to find a way out), to work, and to earn money. For many, farm work is not the aspired center - it is a means to get closer to the center. It is "just a job", a source of income while waiting for a better opportunity.

Vilnord has always been a fisherman and had never done farmwork. He finds it very hard. He misses the sea and wishes that he were back home fishing. He would very much like to find work on a fishing boat like his brother. Vilnord said that he really loves the ocean and feels peaceful only when he is near the sea. But he cannot speak English, and work on a fishing boat is hard to find. His brother told him that commercial fishing in America is very different from the small-scale fishing operations of rural Haiti. While waiting for the right opportunity, Vilnord is biding his time earning money to send home. With the help of his brother, *Bondye bon*, he will get his wish.

Samuel is in America with his six-year old daughter and thirteen year old nephew. Since they arrived together in 1981, he has cared for the children by himself. He takes them with him wherever he goes. They share accommodations with Samuel's brother, Sauveur, in Lake Road Camp. The day I talked to

Samuel, he was feeling sick and his brother was taking
care of him. Although Samuel and Sauveur's situation
seemed unusual, under certain circumstances Haitian
men assume the responsibility for raising their
children. In Haiti, it is culturally acceptable for
men to be nurturing, to show affection to children,
and to care for them. Samuel and his brother were
using Haitian concepts of parenting and kinship in
formulating their strategies.

Although he had worked the land in Haiti, Samuel
says that it is different here.

> In Haiti, you work the land by yourself.
> You are your own boss. You make deci-
> sions, hire people or get help, and in
> return help others. Here you work for
> somebody and he pays you. Working the
> land here is just a job, someone else is
> the boss.

And since he needs money, he says: "I push my body to
its limits". He can fill up to 200 bags on a good day
(earning $50.00 at .25c./ 75lb. bag), and sometimes he
works with a companion. "At the end of the day I can
hardly walk," he says. When the harvest is over he
will go back to Fort Pierce. "As soon as the fruit
season (citrus) starts, you don't even have to look
for a job, you work where you want." He kept his

apartment in Fort Pierce while he was away because he plans to go back there.

Although Samuel finds potato picking a tough job, he came back to Wyoming County because there are good programs for the children during the day. He says that people here (referring to the staff of the BOCES Geneseo Migrant Center) are "honestly interested in us, they understand our problems, our situation. They talk to us, teach us, take us to visit interesting places, and that's why I come back". Samuel's idea of getting to the center is focused on his children. They will be the ones to fulfill his dreams; they will make it even if he cannot.

Some of the Haitians like farm work and are successful workers. Ilmeus is a strong man. He has always worked the land, and he enjoys it. He appreciates being outside and working hard; he can fill 250 to 300 bags of potatoes in a day. Although his aspirations for a better life were being realized, he had already set other goals for himself. He wanted to move to a better-paying crop, apples for example, or form his own crew. Once his center was within reach, he started to *demele*; look for a higher goal and a different center.

Most Haitians think that migrant labor is hard work and hazardous to their health. Yet, though the working and living conditions are poor, and the pay is low, it is sometimes the only opportunity *pou fè yon ti demele*, to earn a few bucks. The immigrants have obligations at home, children and families to support in Haiti. Through their work, their families have a chance to move away from the periphery.

For a few, like Marc, migrant work is not a way to move from the periphery. Marc, who is on his first migrant season, is not making much money on this job. "It's not interesting, it's making me laugh. I can't do it! Not because I am lazy, I'm just not strong enough. Two buckets for a quarter, I've never worked like that here (i.e. in America)!" He lives in Lake Road Camp and averages $20.00 on good days. He had never worked the land in Haiti. In Florida during the citrus season, he works in a packing house making $4.00/hour. "But it is not a steady job, they take people as needed for a week at a time". In Fort Pierce, he lives with a friend, somebody he trusts. He picks oranges sometimes;

> It is a dangerous job, one has to climb
> on a ladder. Some people get hurt, even
> die, and nobody knows that they have
> died. And you can't sue. They just
> take you to a hospital.

Marc's idea of center was <u>not</u> doing farmwork and he was not doing well. In fact, he perceived himself as being in even a more marginal position here. In Haiti, he lived in a city, even if he was not a *moun eklere* (an educated man), he was not a *moun en deyo* (a country man) either.

Work, any kind of work, however, is better than welfare. Even when they are out of work, Haitians do not perceive *welfe* (welfare) as a viable option. They are opposed to it on several grounds, and their refusal reflects Haitian cultural ideas about giving and receiving. Most say that they are guests in this country and "do not want to make trouble," or attract attention. A woman told me that it was not dignified to receive money from people you did not know. Another said that she was told that if she accepted welfare, she would never be able to go back to Haiti, nor write to her children. In the event that she would be granted a residence permit, she would have to pay back all the money she had received, and if she could not, her children would inherit the debt. In general, the migrants believe that it is not good to be on "the dole." The few who accepted public assistance stopped as soon as they found work. Social workers report that in general, Haitians make little use of public assistance programs. They prefer job training, rent subsidies, and will, on occasion, accept food stamps.

Reluctance to accept welfare can be understood in light of the immigrants' experiences in Haiti, as well as in terms of their beliefs concerning giving and receiving. There are no public assistance programs in Haiti. The little amount of foreign aid, mostly from the United States, that reaches the rural areas is given out as food (grains, dried milk, canned goods), agricultural products (tools, fertilizer), medicine, and services (educational and vocational training). At the same time, Haitians believe that no one gets something for nothing, and that people can, and should, make it on their own. This is a central element of *demele*.

The experiences of a number of Haitians, like Charitable, reaffirm their belief in "making it". Charitable is a mild mannered man who looks older than his 39 years. He arrived in America in April 1980, before the Krome detention center was opened. He received assistance during the first six months, but not money he says. He also accepted food stamps

twice. Since then he has been able to *demele ko mwen*
and support himself and his family in Haiti. He lives
a simple life here and does not need much. When he
sends money home, he knows it is spent wisely.

> They buy animals, use it to build
> houses, they don't waste it. My house
> is built, my children are going to
> school. They let me know how they spend
> the money: to buy goats, chickens. Then
> I know how the money was spent. I even
> asked them to buy me a puppy dog.

Charitable's center is still in Haiti. In his case,
the move from periphery to center takes place in
Haiti. He hopes to get back one day to live in the
house that he had built, and to take care of the
animals that were bought with the money that he sends
home.

This was Charitable's first migrant season, the
first time he had come to this "*ladoba de travay sa a*"
(joke of a job).

> Here (in Lake Road Camp) they give you
> filthy mattresses. I would not like to
> take these things to Fort Pierce. We
> have good homes there. The work is also
> bad for your health. You get back-
> aches, breathe dust. I make $100.00/week
> on the average. The other day someone
> stole my savings and my papers too. In
> Florida I can make $300.00 to
> $400.00/week for six months. Then I go
> to contract work. Last year I worked on
> a loader. I earned a little more than
> this; you are paid by the hour.

Though Charitable, like most migrants, is not happy with the working conditions, he is doing it for a specific purpose, to move away from a marginal position.

Conflict resolution: all Haitians are one "_nasyon_"

Haitian rural ideas about the extended family as a unit to resolve conflicts is carried over to their lives in the migrant camps. Quarrels often arise in the migrant camps. Most often these involve individuals, but sometimes the residents are divided into factions around an issue. Conflicts most often arise from inter-personal relations and work related tensions. Haitians are very vocal, and while tempers rise quickly, they are easily dissipated. An outsider witnessing a minor quarrel among Haitians may get the impression that something more serious is taking place. During an argument onlookers are called to give their opinions. Witnesses are asked to join in, litigants can even swear by their ancestral and _vodou_ spirits. These arguments seldom degenerate into fights. It is considered shameful to draw blood from someone. It is a stain on the individual, as well as on the family.

In general, Haitians refrain from physical violence, and conflicts are resolved within the confines of the extended family. The process of conflict resolution requires that an elder or someone of higher status arbitrate a dispute. In the extended family system, kinship ties link individuals and legitimize the role of arbiter. Within the migrant labor system, the camp as a whole functions as an extended family, a fictional kin group. The crew leader (if he is Haitian) and older workers take on the role of mediators, the grower - or any other outsider - is rarely asked to arbitrate a crisis. On the other hand, just like a family, each migrant camp has its own way of handling conflicts, and the quality of leadership influences the atmosphere of a camp.

Lake Road Camp functioned as an extended family. The older woman, Anacia, was treated as a matriarch. One of the older men, nicknamed Dadi, acted as a grandfather. Children were everyone's responsibility. Everyone played with them, fed them, watched them, and disciplined them. The women washed their families' clothes. The older woman often took care of the young

men.   Men as well as women cooked, mostly Haitian
food, and on very few occasions swept the common room.
It is unusual for Haitian men to do housework. It is
considered *travay fanm*, woman's work. But since most
men did not have mates in the camp, they had to perform these chores on their own.

In the absence of an elder kin, a crew leader can
serve as mediator to resolve conflicts. However,
whether or not Haitians will turn to the crew leader
depends on the status they accord him. Yolette's view
demonstrates this choice. Yolette, who lived in Lake
Road Camp, is a very outspoken and strong willed
woman. She says that the *bòs man* lives far from the
camp and that he is not the one who is called to
resolve conflicts. Another migrant worker, Onell, is
supposed to settle differences. But he is inept, she
says, and one is better off calling in the big boss.
In reality, she adds, they settle their own problems
among themselves. Yolette would not even acknowledge
that Onell was crew boss. In her idea of hierarchy,
someone of higher status than Onell should be in that
position.

Marc's opinion confirmed this. He said that there
were two women and a man in Lake Road Camp who helped

resolve conflicts. One acquires status with age;
"they are older, they are wise," he says.

> No one really fights, they scream,
> that's all. There are no major problems
> between the workers and the big boss
> (i.e. grower). The problems are not
> with him (the boss), but in the nature
> of the work.

Marc also believed that most of the conflicts in the
camp were brought about by frustration and tensions,
as well as by the nature of migrant work.

In Jo's Camp there were workers of several ethnic
backgrounds. The Haitians stayed together; they
resolved their differences on their own, adapting
their own cultural values regarding hierarchy, family,
and conflict resolution to solve their problems in the
camps. Even though internal divisions might exist
among the Haitian workers, the group would be united
in its dealings with "the outside," as Jacques' example so vividly shows.

Jacques says that the Haitian workers in Jo's Camp
settled their problems within their group; they kept
to themselves. During the 1982 season, there was a
"macho guy" who liked picking fights. He tried to
fight with Jacques, but the other Haitians intervened.
When I asked him if the crew leader was ever called to
settle these disturbances, he answered, "No. He would

never know. It's not right that a stranger gets involved in internal problems. He would not understand
anyway." He added,

> in case of an argument between Haitians,
> they take care of it among themselves.
> In case of a disagreement between
> Haitians and the boss, the crew boss
> would intervene. If there were problems
> between one Haitian and the boss, the
> others may choose not to work.

This is consistent with the Haitian concept of family
as a self-contained unit, a *nasyon*. In Haiti, family
matters are resolved within the confines of the extended family. In the camps, Haitian matters are
resolved within the confines of the *nasyon* of
Haitians.

Camp life, needless to say, was not all conflict.
There was also harmony. The workers formed a type of
extended family, patterned after the traditional
Haitian rural *lakou* (family compound). They shared
accommodations, spent their leisure time together, and
helped each other.

Nasyon Ayisyen (the Haitian people), reaffirming cultural identity

There is little free time in the camps and there is little to do beside talking, gambling, playing cards, and sleeping. "Here there are no Sundays," said an informant. At the height of the season, the migrants worked all weekend. They used their leisure time to maintain ties with their home communities. This included listening to cassettes of Haitian music and conversations sent to them by their families, playing games like those they used to play at home, telling Haitian jokes and folk tales, and talking about Haiti. Samuel and his brother kept memories of home by telling the children stories about Haiti "so they know where they come from." In this way, the immigrants re-created a Haitian atmosphere while reaffirming the importance of Haitian values in their lives, and transferring them to the younger generation.

When they were not working, said Marie-Therese, people of Lake Road Camp spent time with their friends, and ate together. Frenel loved to tell stories of *Bouki ak Malis* (Haitian folk tales), play *pokino* (a card game), sometimes for money, and play cassettes of Haitian music.

Jean-Robert lived with a group of Haitians in a mixed camp. They prepared Haitian meals together, told jokes, and played games, like dominoes and cards. Sometimes they would sing Haitian songs, and even English ones. However, there was little time for leisure. On most days they left for the fields at seven a.m., to return at six p.m. At the peak of the harvest they would work past nine. Then they had to shower, prepare dinner, and twice a week some would attend English classes. Occasionally, another informant said, he would just bathe and go bed without supper.

Much free time was spent telling stories and folk tales. Storytelling is a great pastime in Haiti. In the camps, joking is an important part of the adaptation process; it mediates between the two worlds in which the immigrants function. Joking acts as a vehicle through which changes are incorporated into the system and are validated. It also reflects the continual assessment of situations in terms of cultural values. The following account illustrates the role of joking in diffusing cultural contradictions.

One evening some outreach workers came to Lake
Road Camp to prepare a spaghetti dinner for the
workers as part of their ESL program (English as a
Second Language). They cooked the food and set the
table with a red and white tablecloth and candles.
During dinner the Haitians were uneasy; either they
may have preferred Haitian food or they did not quite
know how to behave in this particular situation. Yet
they thanked their guests profusely and expressed
their gratitude by telling them jokingly, in halting
English, that it would be great if someone came by
every night to prepare supper. The Creole conversation, jokes and commentaries, however, illustrated the
clash of cultures. It turned out that the Haitians
did not know what spaghetti was, nor how to eat it,
and furthermore, they did not understand the
ceremonial function of candles at an American meal.
Marcelin had everyone in stitches when he asked why
they had to eat by candlelight, since there were no
corpses around. He said that where he came from,
candles are used during *sèvis mò* (service for the
dead), at funerals, or to invoke the *lwa*, *vodou*
spirits. The others answered that if he did not watch
it, the *lwa* would also join us for dinner. All this

joking took place in Creole so as not to offend the benefactors.

Gender relations and _plasaj_ unions: in America there is no good _plasaj_

Relations between Haitian men and women undergo changes in the United States. In rural Haiti, most conjugal unions take the form of _plasaj_. _Plasaj_ is a consensual union sanctioned by the community. It remains a viable strategy for Haitian immigrants in the United States. It is a form of _demele_. However, although the concept remains the same, _plasaj_ has acquired a different meaning in the United States.

Lowenthal (1984) defines the substance of Haitian conjugality as

> that contractual relationship between a man and a woman which links their sexuality and their productivity in what may be, if only in virtue of its explicitness, a peculiarly Haitian innovation in the world of male/female relationships (p 29).

In America this pattern is disrupted. While men and women try to maintain the same kinds of conjugal unions, they find that new factors affect these unions. Familial responsibilities here, as well as in

Haiti, the limited availability of female partners, the absence of support networks, and the demands of life in America limit their range of options.

In the rural Haitian traditional pattern of conjugal relations, value is attached to women's reproductive and productive capacities. The division of labor along gender lines is clear; men work the land and women trade. Women's work is valued; they are economically independent and contribute to the household economy. This economic independence allows them greater freedom to terminate conjugal unions that are no longer productive or satisfactory. The extended family and kin networks also make it possible for women to move back and forth between home and market. Men need women not only to do *travay fanm*, women's work, but also to fulfill their wish for offspring.

In the migrant labor system, women no longer have the same kind of freedom to leave a union. Women have lost their positions as traders, and have to depend on men in the productive sphere; they need them for protection. For men, the situation has also changed. Women have intruded into their traditional sphere of

production - agricultural work. Women are also dissatisfied in their reproductive role. There are no
kin networks here to help them care for their
children.

Women and men see the other gender in the United
States as not performing or conforming to expectations. Men note that there is a difference between
women who emigrated alone and those who came to join a
partner - husband or *plase* - or came with one. The
former are viewed in a negative light in that they
violate expected rules of conduct for women. A man in
Lake Road Camp told me "no real woman makes this trip
alone." Another said, "a good woman should stay home
unless she comes to America to join her man." According to Charitable, "here women are after your money.
They take your money, then they leave you. As soon as
they get to Florida they are *gate*, spoiled. *Lajan
gate yo*, money ruins them."

Women, however, have their own view of Haitian men
in America. The women said that the men they meet
here are not "real Haitian men", that they do not
respect their women and often compare them - in dis-
paraging terms - to the women back home. In Haiti,
they said, "a man will not gossip about a woman with

whom he is living. He will not berate her, or beat
her. Here men speak openly about their mates and often abuse them."

Men and women agree that *plase* unions formed in
America among people who did not know each other in
Haiti are different. "At home", Jean-Juste from Lake
Road said, "*ou konnen*, you know, who you are dealing
with. Here you don't know who they are, where they
come from." One woman, also from Lake Road Camp, told
me "in America there is no good *plasaj*, there are only
boyfriends and girlfriends," and a young man said that
"there is no time for courtship here; things happen
too fast. At home it can take two or three years
before you *konnen*, have relations with, a woman. Here
it happens right away." Innocent said that in Haiti
people form *plasaj* before they get married, "*w ap
eseye fanm nan, avan ou marye avè l. Ou chita avè l,
lè rive yon tan ou wè li bon, ou marye*" (you try the
woman before you marry her. You spend time together,
when you see that it is good, then you get married).

Women in the migrant stream are also unhappy about
their job situation; most of them were traders in
Haiti. At home, they say, farmwork is man's work, not
woman's work. Most Haitian women came to America

believing that they could easily find work as domes-
tics, in hotels or in restaurants. Some women resort
to their traditional women's work as traders and, when
in Florida, engage in petty trade, komès. They buy
fruits and vegetables in bulk and retail them on the
streets or in markets. But this kind of activity is
not very lucrative in the United States. Since rural
women lack education and marketable skills, in America
they are forced into doing farm work which has been
traditionally men's work. Farm work is the only form
of demele they have left. Women have to deal not only
with their own dislike for agricultural work, but also
with the men's resentment. Haitian migrant workers
feel that women are overstepping the traditional division of labor, and that they are intruding in their
sphere of influence.

These tensions arise from the fact that both men
and women feel trapped. Women miss their economic independence and the kin networks that allowed them the
freedom to move back and forth between markets. They
have lost the flexibility to leave a union which is no
longer satisfactory and productive. Women add that
they need male partners to work in the fields. They
cannot lift the heavy bags, but are good pickers.

They also need a mate to protect them from other men. An unattached woman is considered *bouzen*, a promiscuous woman.

Men miss farming their own plots. They say "farm work here is just a job, someone else is the boss." They also lack the sexual freedom allowed them by their culture. Charitable said: "I never had more than one *plase* at a time. I had one woman at a time; if I could not live with her, I would leave her. I would have one wife and *fè afè*, see, others. *Yon sèl dam pa kontente yon gason* (one woman only cannot satisfy a man)." They also say "if you are *plase*, when things go wrong the woman can just go. You can go too." Thus, both men and women find their traditional fields of activity and their conjugal relations transformed and changed according to their view, for the worse.

There are some positive sides to forming unions in the United States. Both men and women believe that a child born in the United States is an insurance against deportation[22]. This perceived advantage is coupled with the traditional cultural values attached to large families. But women who work in the fields, even though pregnant and still caring for younger

children, are often in poor health and depressed.
They are very receptive to the advantages of birth
control methods, but often do not understand the right
way of using them. I found that a woman from Lake
Road Camp was having health problems because she did
not understand the instructions given to her at the
family planning clinic. She was taking two different
kinds of birth control pills while also using other
methods. Depressed, tired, and overburdened by expectations of relatives in Haiti, women often resort to
illegal abortions or other indigenous methods for ter-
minating unwanted pregnancies.

Plasaj remains, however, a viable adaptive
strategy for Haitian immigrants in America; it is a
form of *demele*. The concept remains the same, but it
has acquired a different meaning. Men and women
remain in *plasaj* because of constraints imposed by
their new situations. They need each other to make
it, yet each feels exploited by the other. Childbear-
ing makes the burden heavier for women who find little
optimism in their situation. They have lost their
traditional role in production, their independence,
and their dignity. They find themselves socially,
economically, and emotionally dependent on men.

I suggest that part of the problem lies in the fact that the traditional division of labor has changed. Women have invaded men's sphere of activity. This creates an ambiguous situation for both sexes. But rural Haitian women suffer the greater loss, both in their productive and reproductive roles. Women immigrants have lost the esteem that they had in Haiti, and both men and women see themselves as trapped in situations for which they have no viable solutions. It is not surprising that social workers say that Haitian women seemed resentful, burdened by small children, and generally in poor health, and that men were often unfaithful and unkind to their spouses.

Kinship obligations: *devwa fanmi*

Great efforts go to maintaining communications with relatives in Haiti. Migrants spend large sums on long distance telephone conversations, however, messages recorded on cassette tapes are the main source of news. The immigrants send instructions to those at home about how to distribute remittances, about their whereabouts, and the happenings of the community. Those at home send news of crops, of relatives, and relay messages for people who have left and have not been heard from. Relatives ask the immigrants not to forget their *fanmi*, kin, now that they are doing well in this land of plenty.

Cassette messages help the immigrants maintain social contact with their home communities. Taped messages have much more impact than a letter: the immigrants can hear their relatives' voices, feel closer to them, sing along with them, and participate in a direct way in the life of their family. Tapes can also be played over and over. On the other hand, they can become an added source of stress for the immigrants who are continually and vividly reminded of their *devwa*, obligations, and for the people in Haiti. The lucky ones receive news and money; for the unlucky, there is uncertainty and anger.

The weight of obligations can be overwhelming. The immigrants represent a center for the relatives back home. They are making it, and should be in a position to serve as *patron* to those at home who are in a more peripheral situation. Elius has three children and a wife in Haiti, to whom he sends money regularly. He also supports his mother and an uncle. He is worried because this fall he has not been able to earn much. When he gets to Florida, he will send home what he has managed to save.

Fifty-three year-old Innocent has 13 children, two of whom are in the U.S. Between the three of them, they support the rest of the family and a group of relatives living on the island of La Gonave.

Charitable sends news home both by letter and by cassette. He said, "some things can't be said on cassettes, everyone can hear them. You write a letter for that. I write in French, Creole, anything." When Jean sent money home he would explain on tape how the money was to be divided among his relatives. He also wrote them a letter with the same instructions - so that there would be no mistakes.

The immigrants share their experiences in America with their relatives back home. These stories, in turn, have a great impact on life in Haiti. New ideas and new concepts are transferred to the home community from the guest society. In their messages, relatives ask for a variety of modern gadgets. Cassette recorders, digital watches, and sunglasses are the most requested. Remittances also pay for new homes, fertilizer, farm equipment, and school expenses. The dream of most rural immigrants is to build a good

house in Haiti, pay for their children's education,
and save enough money to go back home.

The immigrants also have obligations in America.
Many have formed new unions here, and their meager
resources have to be spread among both households.
They feel that their economic situation would improve
if they could resolve their immigration status and
have access to better-paying jobs. As legal residents, they would also be able to go home to visit,
and to bring relatives into this country. They often
discussed strategies that could be used to speed up
the process of getting their permanent residence permits. For example, one can contract a *mariaj biznis*,
a business marriage, with an American citizen. In a

> *mariaj biznis ou pa an afe ak moun nan.*
> *Ou pa bezwen rete ave 1. Si moun nan ta*
> *dako ke ou rete ave 1, se yon lot bagay.*
> *Le ou jwen residens ou kite 1.*

> (in a *mariaj biznis*, one does not have
> to be sexually involved with the person.
> You don't need to live together. If the
> person agrees that you live together,
> that's up to both of you. When you ob-
> tain your residence, you leave the per-
> son.)

A *mariaj lov*, on the other hand, is a union between
people who care for each other. Most *mariaj biznis*
among Haitian immigrants are arranged between Haitian
men and American women. They are costly, as well as

illegal enterprises (most women ask a down payment of up to $1,500.00, plus a monthly allowance), moreover, the outcome of such unions is uncertain. The risk, however, is worth taking. It is *demele*, a strategy to help one on the way to making it. The immigrants expressed the hope that "Reagan" would hurry up and do something about their legal status. In their eyes, he _is_ the American government, as Duvalier _is_ the Haitian government.

The power of *konesans* (knowledge)

Haitian immigrants perceive that knowledge of English is important as a way to gain access to a better situation, to move from their actual peripheral position toward the goals they set for themselves. They believe that knowing English and getting an education will enable them to move from periphery to center, to *pouse pi lwen*, go further, and acquire prestige and security. Their prior experience with the linguistic differentiation in Haiti leads them to attribute a great deal of value to the acquisition of languages. In Haiti, language is a social marker: the language one speaks determines his/her position in the

class hierarchy and, by association, economic, political, and educational status. The 15% of the population who speaks French has the monopoly on economic,
social, and political power. For the Creole speaking
rural and urban poor populations, the acquisition of
French is the first step away from marginality. Thus
the immigrants also equate knowledge of English with
upward mobility in the American system.

In Haiti, rural-urban categories are also linked
with Creole-French, uneducated-educated categories.
The acquisition of French is viewed by Haitians as a
way to move from a rural area to an urban milieu, thus
from periphery to center. In America, English acquires the same value attributed to French in Haiti.

Samuel went to school for only two years and he
believes that he would be in a better situation now if
he had had a better education. He says that he is
making sure that his children receive a good education, in order to succeed where he has failed, and to
have a better chance of making it. For him, "there is
no other choice. In this country, if you can speak
English you are OK." He has not been able to learn
English. There is no time for evening classes in his
busy schedule and he thinks that he is too old to

learn. He says that it is easier for him to talk to Black Americans, "they are used to Haitians. You don't need to worry about saying it right, they understand Haitians. With the Whites you have to speak good English for them to understand". Samuel's statement reflects Haitian values regarding language and class hierarchy in Haiti, and their perception of American class system. He is of rural origin and in America, he is also in a rural environment. No English or little English is associated with agricultural settlements, and therefore with other agricultural workers, which, in the case at hand, are also black. Well-spoken English is associated with higher status, and therefore with Whites.

Lorison can write his name and read basic road signs in English. He learned to read in Creole during the two years when he worked days and went to school at night. He always takes part in the camp's classes. He has tried to go to school several times while in Florida. He would attend two or three days, then have to miss because of conflicts with work. He also associates his marginal position in the social hierarchy to his marginal knowledge of English. He does not know much English, just enough to survive. His

several attempts at learning English, and therefore
moving from periphery to center, have been unsuccessful, so he remains in the migrant stream.

Charitable links *konesans*, knowledge, to a greater
understanding of one's surroundings and therefore control over one's life. One with marginal *konesans* can
barely make it, is at the mercy of others, and is des-
tined to remain in a marginal position. He links
konesans with knowledge of French in Haiti and with
knowledge of English in America. Charitable only has
a second grade education; he can barely sign his name
and read. When I asked him why he was wearing glasses
while singing from a hymn book, he explained that he
could make out some of the words. *"Gen kon li pasab,
e gen konesans. M gen konesans. Yo bam yon lèt pou m
al tiye tèt mwen, depi m gade l, m pa prale"* (there is
a difference between being able to read and having a
knowledge of reading, i.e. knowing something about
reading. I know something about reading. If someone
hands me a letter telling me to go kill myself, I look
at it, and I know not to go). He also thinks that it
is important for immigrants to know English in order
to be aware of what is happening around them, and to
be able to do something about it, *"si yon moun pa kon*

pale de mo Angle, ou pa ko menm sou tè a" (if someone is unable to say two words in English [to get by in English], that person is not really in this land).

Religion: *moun ki levangil ak moun ki sèvi lwa* (those who follow the gospel and those who serve the spirits).

Religion was one of the topics most often and most heatedly debated in the camps. The core of the discussions dealt with the relative merits of allegiance to traditional *vodou* gods versus acceptance of Christian faith.

Haitian migrants are aware of the negative values attached to *vodou* both among educated Haitians and among Americans. Thus, through these conversations, they were trying to resolve a moral, as well as a social dilemma. Being a Christian is both a form of *demele* (Christianity may offer an edge against misfortune and they need to take advantage of every opportunity), and, like French, a useful attribute for those trying to cross social boundaries. On the other hand, "*vodou* is part of the country" said an informant, part of the historical and cultural heritage.

When I started fieldwork, no one would admit knowing anything about *vodou*, and even less being a
vodouist, but all were fascinated by the topic. When
asked about their religious affiliation, the answer in
all cases was: "*se moun levangil mwen ye, m pa sevi
lwa*" (I am a Protestant, I don't serve the spirits).
Their conversations, nevertheless, revolved around the
possibility of spirits "crossing the water," the absence of *baka*, *djab* and *lougawou* (malevolent spirits,
demons and witches) in America, personal experiences
with supernatural beings in Haiti, and vodou rituals.
One informant shared with me his bewilderment over the
fact that in America "someone can sit on his doorstep
past midnight without being afraid of being harmed by
roving *djabs*."

Under the practices of *levangil* often lie strong
vodou beliefs. The immigrants' conversations also
revealed that most were trying to come to terms with a
major conflict: on one hand, they had given up *vodou*
worship in favor of the Protestant faith, on the other
hand, they still believed in the power of *vodou*
spirits. To them, the Christian faith was not only a
renunciation of *vodou* faith, but an insurance against

the power of malevolent supernatural beings. They often say "*si ou rantre nan levangil, djab pa kap pran
ou*" (if you convert to the Gospel, the demons cannot
get you).

Lorison told me that some "of those who say that
they are *levangil*" sometimes call a *bòkò* (witch
doctor) to perform certain services for them. But if
someone really believes in God, "if you have faith you
can go to church to the pastor and he will pray with
you and perform a service at your home." However, he
also said, when a farmer plants a garden, even though
he trusts in God, he can also have a service performed
to insure that the garden is good.

During a heated debate, Damier emphatically
stated: "*m pa sèvi lwa*" (I don't serve the spirits),
and that the more he reads the Bible, the more he
realizes that "*vodou* endangers spiritual life." He
explained that ever since he converted, he has not
been ill. He used to get sick very often, and his
parents would take him to see a *bòkò*. He is convinced
that "*le mal existe*" (evil exists, a saying that all
Haitians say in French), but "*si ou pa konn le mal,
moun pa ka fè ou mal*" (if you do not know evil, no one
can harm you). He also believes that spirits can

possess humans, transmit messages, and that they can be sent "over the water" to harm those Haitians living abroad who believe in them.

Other immigrants have a neutral attitude toward the issue. Frenel said that he was not a vodouist. He had heard people talk about *vodou*, but his mother did not want him to know about it. He was baptized Catholic, but does not practice. His rules are few: he knows that God exists, and he will not lie. He adds that some people remember that God exists only when they need him; "If I should die now, I know about God, not only now, but all the time".

MIGRANT WORK IN THE CONTEXT OF ADAPTATION: *YAP DEMELE TÉT YO* (THEY DO THEIR BEST)

Both the data and analysis illustrate that, for Haitian migrant workers, the process of adaptation includes elements of both Haitian and American culture and social structure. This section examines the ways in which Haitian boat people perceive the significance of migrant farm work in their plans for the future.

For Haitians, migrant labor has both a transient and a transitory aspect. The immigrants accept the dismal work conditions and hardship of migrant work because migrancy is one of the ways to achieve their goals. It is a temporary solution, the season only lasts a few months. They complain about the job, time lost to bad weather, and the low pay, but they have to *demele*. They must work hard because of obligations and expectations, and because many people depend on them. Migrant work is an opportunity to earn enough to sustain them until citrus season begins in Florida. Next year one will see what happens; *Bondye bon*, God is good. Therefore, migrant labor is not only tolerated, but is used to one's advantage. *Demele* dictates that one makes the best of a situation. Even those who like farm labor, like Ilmeus, aspire to either work in a packing house, as a loader, or transfer to a more lucrative crop. Others do it until something else comes along. Gesner would like to work in a gas station; Vilnord dreams of being a fisherman. Many wish to settle out of the migrant stream, in a place where there are fewer Haitians.

Three workers elected to stay in upstate New York after the 1983 season, while six had settled in Rochester alone in 1982. No one stayed behind in 1984. Although three contemplated the possibility, and one even tried, at the end of the season they all left for Florida.   They gave different reasons for their decisions.   Henri went back because no one could guarantee that he would find work as a tailor in Rochester.   In Florida, there is always the citrus harvest, and he has several children in Haiti to whom to send money.   Marc was just exploring possibilities; another time, perhaps, he will stay.   Cantave left Lake Road Camp early in September.   An agency had found work for him with a road construction gang in a nearby town.   Two weeks later he was back.   He admitted that he could not stay alone.   There were no other Haitians there, no one to talk to.

The data indicate that as time passes, it becomes increasingly difficult for the immigrants to relocate. In Florida, they have settled into a routine.   Their home communities are now organized, their networks formed, and relationships established.   In previous years they were still flexible.   Moving now would be like leaving home again, and starting the adaptation process all over.

Haitians use the migrant system to their advantage, but the system also affects them.   The migrant farm system is a safe place where one can hide and stay out of trouble, and not attract attention while getting adjusted to life in America. Migrant farm labor is also attractive because it does not require special skills, and most Haitians of rural origins have had some experience with agricultural work. But the unpredictability and disorganized character of migrant life has affected Haitian workers. It has influenced gender relations, personal relationships, and cultural values.

For Haitian boat people, migrant labor is but a temporary and transitory phase. The uncertainty of their legal status underlines their lack of permanence. They wait and hope for legalization of their legal status, for better jobs, to be reunited with their relatives, and for a less marginal position. In the meantime whether migrant labor is to remain a way of life, or to become a step on the way to a better future, *yap demele tèt yo* (they do their best).

An informant summarized what adaptation means for the immigrants when talking about the best way to raise children:

> I have to make them (the children) Haitian and American: they should know where they come from so they can understand their parents; but since they have to live here, they should also learn the American way.

Some migrants took a chance. They broke away from the cycle and stopped following the crops. They stepped into the open and scary space of a big city. The following chapter looks at the way Haitian boat people, and former migrant workers in particular, make it in an urban environment.

URBAN RESETTLEMENT:
IN SEARCH OF BETTER OPPORTUNITIES

POUKISA NOU VINI ROCHESTER (why we came to Rochester)

Most of the immigrants who elected to move to Rochester had a history of rural to urban migration in Haiti. The Rochester population had a higher percentage of Haitians who had either been born in, or later moved to, an urban center than the migrant stream population. Of those interviewed, eight had migrated internally, two were born in an urban area - one in Port-au-Prince - and another had no history of internal migration.

The immigrants believed that they had a better chance of "making it" in an urban milieu. Internal migration had been a successful strategy for most in Haiti, and they expected that it would also work in the United States. The move to Rochester was to be another step in their strategy of upward mobility, in their movement away from a marginal position. At the beginning, their social universe was still anchored in Haiti. They measured their expectations, their accomplishments, and their earnings, in terms of what they had known in Haiti. The longer the immigrants stayed in Rochester, the more I observed a shift away from a Haitian universe toward a more American way of thinking.

Rochester was not the original port of entry for any of the Haitians living in Rochester. A few arrived in this country by plane, the others were boat people. Haitian immigrants living in Rochester explain their decision to settle in the city in a variety of ways. Some came here after long consideration, others did not have the opportunity to make the choice. Marriage, work opportunities, and legal status, as well as a desire to move away from large Haitian communities affected their decisions to settle in Rochester.

Simone did not choose to come to Rochester. Her husband sent for her. He had left Haiti four years before she could join him. They both came on a visitor's permit; now they are illegal aliens. In Haiti they had lived in Port-au-Price. Although they had several relatives in New York City and in New Jersey, her husband felt that he had a better chance of finding work in a city where there were fewer Haitians.

Marcel, Louis, Dieudonne, and Mireille came to Rochester under unfortunate circumstances. A crew leader had promised them work in the apple orchards near Rochester; however, those plans did not material- ize. Instead, they were left stranded in a strange town without any money. They did not know how to cope in the city, did not speak the language and had no idea of what to do next. Several of them went back to Florida. Those who elected to stay made a new life for themselves. Mireille and Dieudonne had always lived in their village. Louis and Marcel had some ex- perience of urban life, *yo se moun provins*, they had lived in small provincial towns. They realized that in Rochester they would have better opportunities to "make it", and better resettlement programs to help them.

Others made the difficult decision to resettle in an urban milieu for other reasons. The decision required careful examination of their situation (economic and familial), an assessment of their skills, of the opportunities the city offered, and an evaluation of their goals. Also they had to leave their "own kind", as Jacques said, and the comfort of familiar surroundings. Those who chose this avenue share several characteristics. They had been urban dwellers before leaving Haiti, had several years of education, some marketable skill (Jacques was a tailor and Yves a welder), and a desire to go beyond just meeting their basic needs. For Haitians, the urban environment is associated with the idea of center, and the rural environment with the idea of periphery. Moving to Rochester was perceived by the immigrants as a move toward a better economic and social status.

Most of the Haitian immigrants who chose to settle in Rochester had also lived in a city while in Haiti. Jacques left the migrant stream to settle in Rochester because he wanted to be in an urban area. In Haiti, he lived in Port-au-Prince and was a tailor. He wanted the opportunity to use this skill here instead of working as a migrant worker. He also associated education with higher social status. He planned to get a high school diploma and enroll in a job training program. Ultimately, he would like to work in a technical field.

The urban immigrants associated farm labor with low status. Jean-Robert always lived in a city. He had been doing farmwork since his arrival in Southern

Florida. In Haiti, he had been a mechanic's appren-
tice and ran a small retail business. Although he
never finished school, he was eager to further his
education. In 1982, he was a migrant farm worker in
Wyoming County, New York. He elected to settle in
Rochester with other Haitian workers. He had found
farmwork difficult,

> it makes you age fast, it's not good for
> your health. Even if you don't feel it
> now, later on it's bound to catch up
> with you. In Haiti, even peasants who
> are used to working the fields age fast.
> They look old, ugly, black. If I had
> worked the land in Haiti, I would be
> even blacker and look older than my 25
> years. Since I worked on the farms,
> I've had pimples, they make me look old.

Jean-Robert's statement underlines black-white
categories of opposition. Haitians use the idiom of
color to convey their perceptions of social
stratification. They associate black with rural and
poor, and white with urban and rich. As one goes up
the social ladder, one becomes less black. Age is
also associated with working the land and being ugly.
In Jean-Robert's perception, poverty is also marginality.

HAITIAN COMMUNITY IN ROCHESTER

The Rochester Haitian community is newly established; it is still being organized, and its history can easily be traced. I estimate that close to 60 boat people had settled in Rochester by 1983. This figure was derived from data collected from my informants and from resettlement agencies. According to the Catholic Family Center of Rochester, at the end of 1985, the Haitian immigrant population had grown to 125 individuals, including about 25 professionals. Between January 1984 and April 1985, this agency alone helped 24 new Haitians coming from Miami. The others came from Haiti and Florida to join relatives and friends.

The present discussion of the "Haitian immigrant community" focuses on Haitian boat people who have settled in the city since 1980. I do not include other Haitians who may have come to Rochester prior to that date, or immigrants from different class backgrounds. The boat people do not represent a community in the sense of an organized interest group or political entity. This study's population is composed of

several clusters of individuals who share similar experiences, backgrounds, areas of origin, and interests. A group of former migrant workers who lived
together for a while belong to the same church, and
keep in close contact; a group of former Ray Brook inmates have shared the same house since their release
in 1982. These and other small groups are scattered
around the northeastern part of the city between the
Genesee River and Culver Road.   There is no formal
network linking all Haitian immigrants, nor any community center where they can meet. A large number of
immigrants attend services at the Parsells Avenue.
Community Church, where a Haitian Pastor conducts portions of the services in French, and occasionally in
Haitian Creole.

There have been several attempts on the part of
community service providers and other Haitian residents to organize community oriented activities. So
far, they have not been successful. This particular
aspect of the Haitian community will be discussed in
more detail later on.

Several agencies are involved in refugee and immigrant resettlement programs within the Rochester

area. Local and State government agencies have assistance programs such as rent subsidies, food stamps,
and job training programs. They fund social programs
run by refugee and immigrant community centers. These
public agencies also fund private organizations that
are designed to facilitate the resettlement process of
new immigrants and refugees. They provide a variety
of programs geared at helping them become self-
sufficient (see Appendix II).

URBAN SETTING: ROCHESTER, NEW YORK

In order to fully understand the problems of
Haitian immigrants in Rochester, their successes, and
the strategies they use to "make it" in this new setting, it is useful to understand some aspects of
Rochester's own social institutions and what the city
has to offer. The socio-economic situation of the
city and its demographic and ethnic composition are
constants, and present a set of constraints around
which the immigrants have to formulate strategies and
goals.

Rochester is the fourth largest city in New York
State. It is located on the Southern shores of Lake

Ontario and is crossed by the Genesee River, which flows northward into the lake.

Rochester's work force is largely composed of highly educated professionals and skilled workers. According to the New York State Department of Labor, the Rochester area has the greatest concentration of high technology employment in New York State. Several light manufacturing companies and a few heavy industries are located within the metropolitan area, but the city's residents are only marginally involved in the several agricultural industries of the surrounding counties. In the larger Metropolitan Statistical Area (the city of Rochester plus five surrounding counties), 4 out of 10 workers are employed in manufacturing. The unemployment rate for the area compares favorably with other metropolitan areas in the state.

ROCHESTER'S TRADITION OF RECEIVING IMMIGRANTS

The 1980 Census reported that the population of Rochester (excluding the suburban areas), consisted of 241,741 inhabitants, 25.8% of whom were Black and 5.4% of Spanish origins. It also pointed out that over the years, several ethnic groups had settled in the city. The large number of foreign-born nationals included in the census revealed that Rochester was still considered as an attractive choice for immigrants coming to the United States.

Italians constitute the largest ethnic group in the city. The majority of the Italian immigrants came to Rochester between 1880 and 1925. By 1920, Rochester had the third largest percentage of Italian-born residents in the United States. They settled in neighborhoods on the East and West sides of town. These same areas had been home to prior immigrants from Ireland and Germany, and today are occupied by Blacks and persons of Spanish origin. Local relief agencies estimate that they have helped 3,700 to 4,500 Southeast Asians resettle in the city since the 1970's. More recently, Rochester has also absorbed refugees and immigrants from Poland, Afghanistan, Ethiopia, Turkey, and several Latin American countries, including Haiti. These new arrivals do not appear in the 1980 Census.

Rochester used to be known for its large clothing industry. At the turn of the century, more than one hundred clothing factories thrived in the city; only one survives today. A succession of highly skilled immigrants from a number of countries provided the manpower necessary to run these businesses. Jews from Eastern Europe fleeing the Austro-Hungarian and Czarist Russian Empires were replaced by other European immigrants, primarily Italians. In the 1970's, Turkish tailors were recruited; then followed Southeast Asians, Rumanians, and other immigrants from England, Ethiopia, Puerto Rico, and Haiti. In many cases, the clothing factories themselves hired immigrants in their homeland and helped them to relocate. Hand-sewing is a difficult skill learned from childhood, and has all but disappeared among the American-born population, and among the population of other industrialized nations. These immigrants did not pass on these skills to their offspring. Instead, they struggled to provide them with an education that would allow them to pursue better-paying and higher status careers. Today, this second generation is employed by high technology companies such as Kodak, Xerox, etc., is in manufacturing, and is running small businesses (Forsyth 1984).

HISTORY OF HAITIAN SETTLEMENT

Until 1980, only a few Haitians lived in Rochester, mainly college students and some professionals. In the summer of 1980, a bus load of Haitian migrant workers was left stranded in the city by a crew leader whose contracts did not materialize. These people found themselves living in an old school bus in the middle of town. They had no money and could not speak English. A few knew some French and were able to communicate with the city's interpreters. The immigrants were temporarily housed at the Triangle Center at the city's expense. They were also registered into public assistance and counseling programs. The media publicized their plight and Haitian residents, as well as local churches and relief agencies, offered to help in the resettlement process. This incident helped to bring the Haitian problem to the attention of Rochester residents. Articles on the influx of boat people in Southern Florida, the detention of undocumented Haitian aliens, and the economic and political situation in Haiti appeared in the local press. In general, public opinion toward the boat people was positive. The numbers were

not overwhelming; only 23 immigrants were involved,
and they appeared to want to be on their own as soon
as possible. By fall, most of the stranded workers
were off welfare, had found accommodations and work,
or were enrolled in job training programs (For a
detailed discussion of the legal status of Haitian immigrants, see Appendix I).

A second group of boat people came to Rochester
after the Ray Brook Detention Center in Watertown
closed down in 1981. Former migrant farm workers and
other immigrants sponsored by resettlement agencies
also chose to settle in the city. These people were
later joined by relatives and friends, some attracted
by the small size of the Haitian community, others by
the economic prospects that the city offered. At this
time, Spring 1986, more than 90% of the Haitian immigrants living in Rochester are employed, and relief
agencies report a low level of welfare dependency
among this population.

However, there have also been some problems. When
the AIDS crisis started in 1983, Haitians were listed
among the high-risk groups. Several immigrants were
fired from their jobs, employers refused to hire
Haitians, and a home-cleaning service run by Haitian

immigrants and sponsored by a local congregation had to close. Haitian immigrants have also suffered from racial discrimination. They avoid any reference to racial and ethnic discrimination, preferring to keep a low profile. During the Summer of 1983, a group of migrant farm workers was again stranded in Rochester after their bus broke down. Most of them were Haitians (Democrat and Chronicle, July 28, 29, 1983). The city of Rochester housed them in a motel in the suburban town of Brighton, an affluent middle class community. The town residents complained about the thirty or so immigrants loitering in front of the motel and frequenting fast food restaurants near the local high school. They feared that these immigrants would break into their homes, accused them of illegal drug dealing, and blamed them for a variety of minor crimes (Personal communication, Rev. Bratton). According to the local police, no Haitian was ever charged of any crime. However, the immigrants did violate city and fire codes by loitering in front of the motel and cooking meals in their rooms. After several weeks, all the occupants were forced to evacuate the area (Personal communication, Pastor Bratton).

MEETING THE HAITIAN ROCHESTER COMMUNITY: *NASYON AYISYEN-NASYON AMERIKEN* (Haitian people-American people)

My first meeting with the Rochester immigrants serves to highlight several Haitian categories of opposition, as well as the concerns of the Haitian community. It was the only event attended by a cross-section of the Haitian community during my fieldwork. Until then I had met some of the immigrants on an individual basis or in small groups. Jacques, a former migrant worker, helped me contact the Haitians and organize the meeting in a local church. Eighteen people attended the meeting.

When I arrived, Jacques was already standing in front of the church with three other Haitians. He was dressed in a suit and carried a briefcase. Acting as coordinator of the event, Jacques welcomed me in English, showed me a list of the people he had contacted, and informed me of the latest developments. Since we had already discussed all that by telephone in Creole and the others could not speak English, his choice of English was significant. He was signaling to me and to the others that he considered himself a *moun eklere* (an educated man). His knowledge of

English gave him higher status among the other Haitians, some of whom he considered *moun sòt* (uneducated). It also pointed out that Jacques wanted to underline his social status. In Haiti he belonged to the urban Class III, and knew how to function in an urban environment. Having made his point about his social position, he switched into Creole and invited the others to join in the conversation.

I went in with our guests to arrange chairs for the meeting while Jacques, who acted as host, stayed outside to welcome the others. Before the meeting started, I spoke with those whom I already knew and took down the names of the participants and other relevant data.

I introduced myself to the group in Creole, although I knew that some of those present would understand French. However, by using French, I would have established a social gap between the immigrants and myself. For similar reasons, Jacques did not use French at the meeting either. The use of Creole conveyed that here, in America, we were all equally Haitians.

I explained my research project, telling them that I wanted to write about how Haitian boat people "make it" in the United States, particularly migrant farm workers and boat people living in Rochester. They agreed to help and thought that it would be a good opportunity to present "a true picture of who Haitians really are". Everyone wanted to express an opinion and had a point to make.

Urban immigrants are more aware of American public opinion of Haitians than are migrant farmworkers. This awareness generated concern and a desire to deal with the negative image of Haitians presented by the media. Their readiness to assist me has to be seen in this light. They hoped that I would write something that would present what they perceived to be a true image of Haitians. They were concerned that Haitians have "a bad image in this country" and that it hurt them in terms of jobs, pride, and dignity. They believed that "a few Haitians who are actually 'bad' give a bad name to the whole group".

They also talked about AIDS, since in 1983, Haitians were still among the high-risk group together with homosexuals and intravenous drug users. They thought that those Haitians who had AIDS should divulge their involvement in homosexuality or drug use, so as to clear the name of the group (in Haiti

homosexuals are considered misfits and are shunned).
They seemed to have followed closely the press and TV
coverage, and were interested in the statistical distribution of the high-risk groups.

In an effort to dissociate themselves from a negative public image, they talked about their attitudes
towards alcoholism, crime, and drug abuse. They said
that they could not understand how people could enjoy
being drunk, and pointed out that there are few
drunkards on the streets in Haiti. They were very
critical of Black Americans. They believed that one
should always be clean, even if poor, and that Black
Americans look clean only when they have money.

Haitian and American families are different according to Haitian immigrants. They perceived
Americans as lacking family unity. Parents and
children do not live in harmony, and family conflicts
are not kept within the family. They told several
stories of their experience, and two will serve to illustrate their views. Jacques talked of a young white
man living in his building who was always drunk and
broke. He constantly quarreled with his parents who,
although well off, did not take care of their son.
Dieudonne told the story of a young woman (nineteen

years old) who constantly argued with her parents and
even called the police during one of these arguments.
To involve the police in a family quarrel was ab-
solutely incomprehensible to Haitians.   Fritz noted
that he had lived with his parents until he left
Haiti, at the age of twenty-five.   The consensus was
that parents and children should respect each other
and live together in harmony.   Even though tensions
always exist between them, one should not turn against
the other, and familial problems should be resolved
within the family.

The discussion in the meeting also highlighted
relations between the immigrants and their relatives
in Haiti, as well as their responsibilities toward
them. They talked about remittances and stressed that
those who worked had to help those in need. They
pointed out that they had not observed this kind of
mutual help among Americans.

The immigrants saw a link between economic
hardship and political oppression. The political
situation in Haiti, in their view, fostered the poor
economic situation of the country.   Most said that
they would gladly go back if the political situation
was better.   They were proud of their country, its

history and natural resources, which they greatly exaggerated.   They claimed that few foreigners really
know Haiti and that those who do, like it and respect
its people.   They alluded to "some aspects of Haitian
culture," meaning *vodou* that are misinterpreted and
contribute to the negative image of Haiti in America.
The urban immigrants were definitely more attuned to
the host society's views of Haiti.   They were concerned that some people made negative generalizations
from the observation of isolated facts.

Although the employment picture was not very positive in 1983, the immigrants were taking advantage of
several opportunities that Rochester offered.   Six immigrants present at the meeting were unemployed, only
two worked full-time, and the others had part-time
jobs (some held more than one).   Four had gone through
a job training program, and two were still in one.
One person was in food services, and the other in
trucking.   One was on welfare.   Few were enrolled in
ESL classes.

The lack of unity among these urban immigrants
stands in sharp contrast to the unity within each
group.   The various groups often reflect different
regions in Haiti.   The four participants (three men

and one woman) belonging to the 1980 group of resettled migrant workers, came from the same area in Haiti. They said that their group still kept in close touch, and several actually shared housing. They met often, attended the same Church on Parsells Avenue, and celebrated holidays together. They did not have much contact with other Haitians living in Rochester. The three former Ray Brook inmates came from the same region on the southern coast of Haiti. They had been in detention together, and elected to settle in Rochester where they shared a house. The seven former migrant workers from Wyoming County formed a tight-knit group. They participated in ESL programs, belonged to the same church on Andrews Street, and four shared an apartment on South Clinton. They had never met any of the other Haitians present. Three of the four others (a woman with a baby and the only couple present) lived in an apartment near Bay Street. They also belonged to the Parsells Avenue church. They seemed to be in a different category: the women had come by plane to join their husbands.

This was the Haitian community of Rochester as I met it in August 1983. By the end of my field work in March 1984, many changes had taken place.

THE ADAPTATION PROCESS

The Haitian immigrant community of Rochester is very different from other Haitian communities in the United States. It lacks the social diversity of the New York City population, the home-like atmosphere that the ethnic enclave of Miami offers, as well as the anonymity and isolation of the migrant farm labor camps and the agricultural communities of southern Florida. On the other hand, Rochester offers different kinds of opportunities. There are few illegal and undocumented aliens, and the employment rate is high. The small size of the Haitian community itself is an opportunity - immigrants are not bound to a community and have more freedom to join the mainstream of American society.

Ki jan nou demele nou (how we "make it")

The employment rate among Haitian boat people in Rochester in 1986 is now over 90%. Most of the immigrants are employed in the service sector. They work as janitors, in restaurants, hotels, and hospitals. A few are blue-collar workers employed in clothing factories as tailors, glove makers, and in industry as welders and assembly-line workers. Most of them hold more than one job.

The picture was not always so bright. The immigrants had great expectations. In the beginning, they were not very realistic. Their perceptions of employment opportunities did not always correspond to their qualifications. Several became discouraged and returned to Florida. Those who remained were determined to "make it". *Demele* and the expectations of relatives helped them to persist. They *debat* (struggled) and tried a variety of options. Some found their niches, others are still *bat kò yo* (trying, making an effort). The winters were also difficult and did not help the lonely ones. Victor used to be very depressed,

> *M te konn pensione lakay mwen.*
> *Menm maŋge m pat ka maŋge,*
> *menm bwe m pat ka bwę,*
> *menm domi m pat ka domi,*
> *telman map krie, telman map pensione*
> *madanm mwen ak manman mwen.*

> (I used to think of home.
> I could not even eat, I could not even
> drink, I could not even sleep because I
> cried so much, because I thought so much
> about my wife and my mother.)

The immigrants used a variety of strategies to "make it" in the city. These strategies reflected the influence of unique factors operating in Rochester, and the more general conditions that the immigrants shared, as well as Haitian cultural ideas. Often what seems like aberrant behavior can be understood when the underlying reasons are brought to the surface.

✳Yves came to America in 1977. He had no legal documents until 1981, when he presented himself to the INS with other boat people and was issued an I-94. Before that he used to go from place to place, sneaking his way into low-paying jobs, and living with relatives. In 1982, he joined the migrant stream, and decided to remain in Rochester to find work as a welder. Yves' constant moving was a form of *demele*, a way of dealing with his illegal status. He was forced to change location and accept low-paying jobs in order to avoid detection by immigration officials. On the other hand, he was able to take advantage of connections within the Haitian community in order to find housing and information about prospective employers.

Other barriers, such as the lack of English and lack of job qualifications confronted the immigrants. Even though Michel and Simone had skills, (he is a

tailor and she is a dental hygienist), it was difficult for them to find work in their fields. In order for Simone to work as a hygienist in America, she
would have had to take a refresher course and pass a
state exam. But she could neither afford the cost of
tuition, nor speak the language. Instead, she had to
settle for work in a glove factory.

Haitians' strategies for success in Rochester depended on the maximization of every opportunity that
the American system and the city had to offer. The
Haitians took advantage of programs and services made
available by social and resettlement agencies: rent
subsidies, employment, job training, and counselling
programs. This is *demele*, to make the best of every
opportunity. It is the Haitian way. This cultural
trait, coupled with individual determination, helped
them to move closer to their goals and their centers.

It took a year before Jacques could finally work
as a tailor. After leaving the migrant stream, the
Geneseo Migrant Center put him in touch with Rural New
York Farmworkers Opportunity, which was to help him
resettle. He received rent subsidies and the choice
of job training or job searching assistance. However,
he felt that the resettlement agencies were too quick

to put people on welfare, instead of giving them proper counseling. He believed that more counseling would have helped him avoid later mistakes. The idea of receiving financial assistance from the state is not a Haitian way. It is contrary to the spirit of *demele*.

In some instances, Haitian cultural ideas, individual effort, and opportunities that the American system has to offer, came together. Jacques took advantage of every opportunity. He accepted help from resettlement agencies and social services, but some of his personal qualities contributed to his success. He also experienced the limitations of the system, such as color and competition in the work place.

When I met Jacques in 1983, he was working a few hours a week as a gas station attendant, and in a restaurant as a dishwasher, when they needed extra help. He had lost a good job in a factory. The employer said that he slept on the job. He claimed that he was fired because he was Haitian and black. During this initial period, he attended ESL classes and was actively searching for better opportunities by going over the "want ads" in the local paper and visiting employment agencies. In August 1983, he realized his goal and was hired as a tailor. He has since received a promotion and several raises. He also came across difficulties. He thinks that he is a good tailor but, "because I sewed something a different way I was suspended from work. My way was better and the supervisor was jealous. They called me back the next day." He still attends evening classes and plans to go on for training "in computers" in case he loses his tailoring job. He also works part-time in a local hospital[23].

Salomon also took advantage of what America has to offer. He was another one of the seven former migrant farmworkers helped by Rural New York. He says that the agency gathered information on each of the seven immigrants in order to better help them. They stayed several weeks in hotels, then moved to their own homes. Salomon tried several avenues. He went into a job training program for three months, he started in cleaning services, then changed to electronics. He was paid while in training, but spent three more months looking for a job. During that time he received help from Social Services. But Haitian ideas of *demele*, to "make it" on one's own, were also

important to him. As soon as he got a job, he can-
celled his welfare and wrote the letter himself. He
was proud of being able to be part of the system by
writing to the Department of Social Services in
English, on his own. He finally found work in a
hotel, but left Rochester in 1984, to join his brother
in New Jersey, after an affair with an American woman
ended on a sour note.

At times everything seems to go well for immigrants. They are at the right place at the right
time and are able to take full advantage of available
opportunities. Luc was a welder in Haiti, he lived in
a small town. When he left the migrant stream, one of
the local agencies found him work in his field, in a
factory. He is young, energetic, and is well-liked in
his job. He has been able to place four more Haitians
in similar jobs. This has given him a great deal of
status with the other immigrants, and he is also proud
of his achievements. His *mariaj biznis* was successful
and he became the first Haitian immigrant in Rochester
to receive permanent residence status. His next goal
is to get married.

In many cases, more than determination was necessary for one to use the system successfully. Adaptation was difficult for immigrants from rural backgrounds who lacked skills and education. Ti-Jeanne
arrived in Rochester in 1981; she was then in her
early fifties. She was one of the workers stranded in
Rochester. She had no history of internal migration
in Haiti, and was overwhelmed by the complexities of
life in the city. At first she had trouble finding a
permanent position. She was a middle-aged woman with
no education or skills, and she did not speak English.
She was hired by a dry cleaning service for a few
weeks, but could not cope. In the fall, she went to
pick apples in Wayne County. That did not work out
very well: she hurt herself on a ladder. She finally
found work at the clothing factory pressing finished
garments. She stayed about two years until they had a
lay-off. Now she is again unemployed and worries
about her children and relatives in Haiti. She had to
accept welfare and felt bad about it. Her rural background did not prepare her for life in a city. Her
age was also another negative factor; she no longer
had the energy and the ability to "make it".

"Making it" depends on several factors, some of which have already been mentioned. In addition, social and structural barriers that the immigrants encounter in this country force them into occupations and statuses of lower prestige than what they had in Haiti. Emanuel is a very angry and dissatisfied man. He claims that he is in this country because he had no other choice. He speaks English well and has had a good education; in Haiti he was a school teacher. He had to leave the country for political reasons in 1980, and ended up in Rochester in 1983. He has trouble keeping a job. He worked briefly in a downtown hotel, but left because he felt discriminated against and because he was refused time-off to get married. He then worked as a nursing assistant, then left to go to the local community college. He started studying Electronics, but now would like to switch to Human Services. He is also trying to get a part-time job during the day in order to attend evening classes.

"Making it" in the city

    Haitian immigrants were often overwhelmed by the
complexities of life in Rochester. Banking, account-
ing, and monthly budgeting were new to most of them.
In Haiti, workers are usually paid in cash, and no
money is withheld for taxes, medical insurance, etc.
In the rural areas, bartering is still practiced,
reciprocal obligations often take the place of cash
payments, and informal borrowing is common especially
among relatives. What appeared as large sums of
money, by Haitian standards, would not stretch far
enough in Rochester.   There were remittances to be
sent home, *bil* to pay. On payday they would be disappointed because they had not taken account of deductions. I was often asked to explain telephone bills,
interest on credit purchases, bank statements, sales
taxes, and deductions on pay check stubs.

    The immigrants lived frugally. Their first
priority was to accumulate enough money to be used in
case they were out of work, or to help family members
emigrate. They were fascinated by gadgets (watches,
tape recorders, televisions, etc.), and cars. One of
them has managed to save enough for a down-payment on

a house. He plans to rent rooms to other Haitians to help pay the mortgage. He found that he could take advantage of other opportunities that the American system offered. In Haiti, these opportunities are unavailable to people of his social status.

The immigrants learned many rules the "hard way". One informant was arrested when his neighbors called the police because he had clipped his dog's ears himself. The man was very disturbed. He had taken care of his animals in his village in Haiti, and could see nothing wrong in doing the same thing in his apartment in Rochester. Another did not know the penalties involved in driving without a license, or proper insurance, until he was stopped by the police and fined.

The immigrants tried to explain new situations in light of familiar Haitian experiences. One told me of an exciting experience he had. He had been to a shopping center where there was a computer. For a quarter, plus the date of birth, it produced a profile of the individual's character. So he put his money and entered his date of birth and received his paper. He was very surprised by the result, and told me "the computer is like a bokò (witch doctor, diviner); it told me the truth about myself". In his perception, the computer, like the diviner, can deal with the world of things unseen.

Conflicts often arise among members of a group and they are resolved in a variety of ways. Following the Haitian custom of resolving conflicts within the extended family, most quarrels are settled within the co-residential group. When this strategy fails, outsiders are called in to arbitrate the dispute. Most often a clergyman, someone from one of the resettlement agencies, or another Haitian (an elder or someone of higher social status in the Haitian community), will be asked to give an opinion. In this case, the outsiders function as a fictive kin group whose ties extend beyond the community.

Some of the conflicts are generated by social tensions, as in the case below that illustrates how Haitian ideas of hierarchy, and the oppositions of rural:urban and *moun sòt-moun eklere* are expressed. Jacques and Luc shared an apartment with Salomon on the East side of town. They had a longstanding argument and each one asked me to listen to his side of the story. Jacques was angry at his housemates; he said that they were not the kind of people with whom he wanted to live. He was from Port-au-Prince and

considered the others as *moun mòn*, uneducated
peasants. He complained that they were loud, charged
long distance calls to his account, and never paid
him. In general, he claimed, they had no desire to
better themselves. They only pretended to be *levangil*
(People of the Bible, i.e. Protestants) to please the
pastor who had helped them. In reality, they were
vodouists. As soon as he had enough money, he rented
his own apartment. He signaled his Class III status
by "moving out of Clinton and up to Meigs;" the other
side of town. Jacques considers himself a *moun eklere*
(educated person) and would like to break all ties
with those he considers *moun sòt* (stupid, uneducated
people). He told me that Salomon and Luc, as well as
Fritz and Pierre who live next door, did not know how
to act responsibly. They distrusted him because he
had a good job, is doing "OK", goes to church, speaks
English, and goes to school.

> They are jealous, but they cannot see
> that mine is the right way to be
> successful in this country. They go to
> church, but only pretend to be Chris-
> tian. In Haiti these men were nothing,
> and they will amount to nothing here.
> They don't believe in the Bible.

A few months later Jacques told me that he was again
seeing his old friends. He was lonely and homesick

and had no one else to turn to. He said: "They are
OK. From time to time you need your own people, your
own language." Jacques, like other socially mobile
immigrants, was caught in a dilemma. On one hand he
wanted to maintain the class distinctions that existed
between him and his friends in Haiti, on the other
hand he realized that in America they all shared their
Haitian identity. Luc and Salomon wished to emphasize
the idea of sharing that exists in extended families
in rural areas; Jacques' strategy depended more on individual achievement.

Others who come from rural areas (Class IV) do not
emphasize social distinctions, even when they achieve
a measure of success. Luc is a jolly fellow, he comes
from a rural area. He has been successful, he had a
good job and had acquired a great deal of prestige
among the immigrants. He had found work for three
other Haitians in the factory. His status here
reflects his achievement in America. He was not interested in maintaining the rural-urban distinctions
like Jacques. He said "Jacques pretends to be Christian, but in reality he sleeps around. He talks a lot
about the Bible, but does not practice what is in it."
He understood that Jacques needed to be with other

Haitians and said that "Jacques was just excited, when
he calms down he will be back".

On the whole, life in an urban center is rather
bleak for the immigrants. They work hard, and several
hold two jobs. They are under a great deal of pressure from their families back home, and have little
time for leisure. They suffer from loneliness, miss
their relatives, and are torn between struggling to
"make it" in this country and going back home as
failures.

Jacques would like to bring his wife to Rochester.
Between the two they "could pull others", his brother-
in-law and nephew for example. This is the Haitian
way: together they can "make it". Under the circumstances, this is also the only way for him to see
his children. He misses them, but is torn between
going home and not being able to return to the United
States. The American system offers many opportunities
that he would like exploit. If they were all here and
working, they could buy a house. They could rent
rooms to other Haitians. At present, he is lonely and
frustrated. Other barriers come into play. If the
wife cannot come, he could get married, but "there are
no available Haitian women in Rochester." So far he

only had white girlfriends. He is afraid of Black
American women. This attitude also reflects his social aspirations.

Some goals are shattered on the verge of being
realized. *Demele* strategies are not enough to deal
with some of the barriers that the American system imposes. Hippolite is a young man. He had a good job
here and was excited at the prospect of seeing his
wife again. They had been married shortly before he
left Haiti in 1981. He had managed to send her enough
money to get a passport and a tourist visa (it cost
her $2,500). When she landed at Kennedy Airport in
New York, a suspicious immigration officer found her
marriage certificate in her suitcase. "They" decided
that she had come with the intention of overstaying
her visa and "she was put in jail for a year." At the
end of the year she was sent back to Haiti. Hippolite
managed to get to New York four times to visit her
before she left. He was shattered, everything around
him had collapsed. He suffered a mental breakdown and
it will be a long time until he recovers. His doctors
say that he will be unable to work for another year.
The INS is the main obstacle with which Haitian immigrants must deal. It represents the other side of

America. On one hand, America offers a variety of opportunities, on the other, it imposes insurmountable
barriers.

Nasyon Ayisyen nan Rochester: Haitians in Rochester

There is no organized Haitian community in
Rochester. The immigrants deplored the situation, yet
no one attempted to solve the problem.

The way Haitian immigrants organize themselves
here is similar to the way Haitians are organized at
home. The concept of community is closely linked to
that of "family". In Haiti, the family is composed of
individuals linked by different kinds of kinship ties
that may extend over several locations, even outside
the country. For Haitians, "family" includes a range
of kinship and fictional kinship ties that can be ac-
tivated for reciprocal support. The extended family
structure is the basic unit of social organization.
It is the locus of all decisions for its members. Individual decisions are most often made in the context
of family-based strategies for survival and continuity. Outside the family lie the various political
and economic systems that affect it (Fjellman and

Gladwin, 1985). The Haitian family has been able to
survive oppression and poverty by taking advantage of
reciprocal obligations and *demele*[24]. Talking about
the members of his family, an immigrant said: "*si youn
gen de pias, ou konnen tout gen de pias*" (if one has
two *pyas* - unit of currency - you know that all the
others have the same amount). The immigrant is in
this country on behalf of his extended kin group. As
a family member is settled, he or she helps another.
The family is a *nasyon* (autonomous group, nation);
what happens inside the family is not discussed outside of it.

Haitian immigrants living in Rochester try to re-
create a similar structure. Although kinship ties are
replaced by other kinds of bonds, the co-residential
unit functions like an extended family.

Jean-Robert does not associate with many Haitians,
only the former migrants who moved here at the same
time. There are three of them in the same house.
Sometimes they play Haitian music. On Sundays they go
to church, watch TV, and take walks. When I asked him
if he knew the other Haitians living in Rochester, he
answered:

> I've seen them. I don't know where they
> live. The Haitians here have no real
> relations, they do not get together like

> those in New Jersey, Miami, New York.
> When there are many Haitians in a com-
> munity they visit each other.

There is no Haitian community here because "..there
aren't many Haitians, a few here and there, spread
about the city, they have no 'ako' (harmony)."

Jacques said that:

> Haitians are egoists, they cannot get
> together to form a community. They will
> only accept leadership from someone of
> higher status. Someone who has an of-
> fice (a title), but just any little guy
> cannot assume leadership.

In some cases, kin ties reach out beyond a single
group to include clergymen, social service providers,
and other Haitians with whom the immigrants had close
contact during their initial resettlement period.

Simone had a few Haitian friends, especially those
who shared her apartment and the owner of the house
they lived in. She said that she knew of other
Haitians and had met several new people at the meeting
in August. There were several men she did not know.
They keep mostly to themselves. She knew two groups
who frequented the Parsells Avenue church.

> The Pastor is very helpful to Haitians,
> and he lives near the church. There is
> a Haitian Pastor who lives in the Par-
> sells Avenue house (members of the 1980
> group). He was sent to Bible school by
> the Church and has some kind of certifi-
> cate. Sometimes both pastors perform
> the service. Sometimes they divide the

congregation; the Haitians go together.
We sing in Creole and in French. The
Pastor preaches in French, and we pray
in French.

The use of French during these services lends an

official character to the Haitian congregation. It

also reflects the fact that other Haitians of higher

status also attend these services. The size of the

congregation varies from a few to twenty. "A lot come

at holiday times. Several work on Sundays". Simone

mentioned that the Haitians would like to form a con-

gregation of their own, with their own pastor. They

could spend more time together. But the community is

not ready to make that move. "A retired colonel (of

the Haitian Army) who is active in the Church started

a small school there for Carbines", but few attended.

The group of immigrants who were helped by Rural

New York often referred to it as "my family". Rural

New York "socialized them", counseled them, and helped

them find jobs. The label "my family", implies

obligations on both sides. The immigrants will always

be grateful, and owe allegiance to the agency. On the

other hand, they expect it to provide help and sup-

port. Referring to a lawyer who has helped him, an

immigrant said "he is my heart". In some ways, this

fictitious extended family structure, which the immigrants create, slows the formation of an integrated
Haitian community. But as the immigrants talk about
and meet to discuss the lack of community feeling and
harmony, they are in fact creating a community. They
are making new acquaintances, bridging lines of
cleavages between the groups, and building networks.

Black-white categories of opposition: a Haitian perspective

In general, Haitian immigrants in Rochester
refrain from discussing problems related to racial and
ethnic discrimination. They recognize that Haitians
encounter discrimination, yet they are reluctant to
discuss the issue. Some choose to ignore or minimize
discrimination, and claim that as guests in this
country, they have no right to judge it. Pastor Belcher of the Community Bible Church of Rochester mentioned noted that in his community there was a great
deal of friction between Haitians and Black Americans.
The Haitians viewed Black Americans as people who
drink excessively and gamble. The Black Americans

resented the help and attention the Haitians are getting, as well as their attitude toward work. They
claimed that Haitians were taking jobs away from them.
The Pastor mentioned a few examples of discrimination
against Haitians. One involved a Black American who
had been evicted from his apartment on Harris Street.
He blamed two Haitian neighbours and attacked them.
Pastor Belcher also supported Jacques' claim that he
had been fired from his job because he was Haitian.

Jacques was the one who talked the most about racial prejudice. He attributed his failure to obtain a
residence permit to the fact that he is black. He
claimed that he had never experienced racial prejudice
before coming to this country. *"Afè nwa pa gen valè
nan peyi icit* (a black man is not valued in this
country). But it's their country so what can one do?
It's hard to be black; whites have no problems." He
was constantly reminded at work that he is black. A
workmate called him "blacky". He believes that those
who judge others on the basis of color and use *avantaj
koulè* (color as an asset) to claim higher social
status, are *moun sòt* (stupid people). He will not let
their attitude weaken his resolve. Instead, he takes
refuge in the Bible and believes that God is on his

side, "*kolè Bondye se dife*" (God's anger is like fire).

Most of the others echoed Jean-Robert's feelings. He said that he had not experienced discrimination because he did not live with *etranje* (foreigner i.e. someone he does not know). He added:

> When you are a guest in someone else's country, there are certain things you should not do. You should not attract attention to yourself. When you know the situation: you are black and a foreigner, and that even the *pitit peyi yo* (sons of the country, i.e. citizen) who are black are looked down on, you stay aside. If the Black does something you do not approve of, do not applaud him so that you are not assimilated with him and receive more humiliation.

Haitians complain of social discrimination more than of color prejudice. Americans who are involved with Haitians support this interpretation. Nyla Gaylord, of Rural New York Farmworkers Opportunities, commented that the immigrants had a strong sense of self-worth and could not accept the fact that they were victims of color prejudice. They saw themselves as forced to be part of a sub-culture that they did not respect and that did not respect them. They perceived themselves as worthy individuals forced by circumstances into a status they considered inferior. They did not seem to have problems relating to whites, and did not always recognize prejudice. She believed that they were real survivors; "just coming here is a screening process."

Both Jacques' and Ms. Gaylord's comments reflect a paradox of Haitian culture. In Haiti, there is no racial prejudice at the ideational level, while at the structural level, color is used as a class marker. While racial prejudice is culturally not acceptable, social and class distinctions are often based on skin color. The distinction is not grounded on a belief that a difference of cognitive potential exists between races, or that any one racial group is inferior to another. However, color is used as a metaphor to talk about social hierarchy.[25]

Haitian immigrants were often angered by the negative image that Americans have of Haiti. They felt that their history, culture, and values were being ignored. Instead, their illegal status in this country, their race, and the fact that they came from an impoverished nation were being emphasized. Emanuel said that Haitians were at the mercy of others because Haitians are poor and malnourished. He wanted to form

a coalition of Haitians to improve the image of Haiti, organize a propaganda blitz to gain respect for Haiti and Haitians. *Ou pa gen pou bay pov, men pa*

crache sou li (you don't have to feed
the poor, but don't spit at them
either).

Levangil: a strategy to move away from marginality

Religion was an important component of Haitian
immigrants' lives in Rochester. At first, all the immigrants denied knowing anything about *vodou* or having
any ties with it. When we became more comfortable
with each other, and they realized that I was not
judging their religious beliefs, they would speak
about *vodou*.

Most belonged to a congregation, attended Sunday
services, and had received some form of assistance
from various Protestant or Catholic groups since their
arrival in the United States. Several said that they
had been baptized in the Catholic Church, and later
become Protestants. In Haiti, the Catholic Church is
the state church and most Haitians, urban and rural,
are baptized Catholic. However, *vodou* is widely practiced, specially in the rural areas, often alongside
Catholicism. On the other hand, Catholicism is practiced by most urban residents. Members of Class III

who need to break away from traditional peasant practices in order to distance themselves from rural backgrounds, look at conversion to Protestant churches as
a way to accomplish their goals, as a strategy.

> While conversion is highly individual-
> ized, in practice it often serves as a
> collective response to hardship... Most
> conversion accounts show practical con-
> siderations to be more significant than
> a crisis of conscience (Smucker 1984:
> 52).

Religious affiliation reflects the transitional
character of Class III. They are neither rural, nor
yet completely urban; they are in-between the two
categories, possessing some of the characteristics of
both.

Protestant churches have established several missions in Haiti. They have been very successful, especially in rural areas where they offer medical services and organize educational and economic development
programs (Smucker 1984). Converts said that *moun
levangil* (people of the Gospel, a term used to
describe Protestants) are asked to renounce their ancestral gods and "the worship of Satan". In return,
the Church promises the certainty of a place in heaven
and protection against evil in this life. The immigrants expressed their beliefs that *"moun levangil*

*pa nan djab. Si ou rantre nan levangil djab pa ka
pran ou. Cris pi fò pase djab. Le mal existe*" (those
of the Gospel are not with the devil. If you become
levangil, the devil cannot get you. Christ is
stronger that the devil. Evil exists).

Aside from their spiritual messages, Protestant
missions also offer practical benefits. Through
health care, educational, and job training programs,
they project the image that *moun levangil* also have a
better chance of "making it" in this world if they
renounce *vodou*. For many Haitians, conversion to a
Christian faith was a strategic choice, a form of
demele, a way to move from periphery to center. It
was both an insurance against adversity, and an opportunity to move toward better economic and social positions. In a society where literacy, the command of
French, and Christianity are so closely linked to
higher social status, membership in a Protestant
church is considered an important step toward upward
mobility.

For rural Haitians, *vodou* is not only a religion,
it is an integral part of social organization. It is
also folklore, music, folk medicine, family tradition,

productivity of the land, agriculture, etc. Therefore, it is not easily eradicated. Underlying Christian practices lie traditional cultural patterns and
beliefs.

Robert's statement on this particular point is
very illuminating. He said:

> In Haiti, *vodou* is part of the country.
> If you want to go see, you go. You grow
> up with *vodou*, and some like it, but it
> gives the country a bad name. It helps
> some. Since Haiti is a poor country,
> the bad side of *vodou* is emphasized. If
> we were rich, people would not bother
> us, they would leave us alone.

Salomon said "..I know two countries. You are either
with God or you are with the *boko*.

In reality, two systems of beliefs operate among
Haitians of Classes III and IV, even after conversion
to *Levangil*. Although they give up the practice of
vodou, they still retain some of its beliefs. Simon's
case illustrates this ambivalence and the degree to
which *vodou* beliefs permeate social life in rural
areas. Simon was baptized Catholic, later became
Levangil, and now belongs to a Protestant church in
Rochester. Three of his mother's brothers were
Protestant pastors, one in Haiti, one in Nassau, and
one in Miami. Simon suffered from a nagging backache
that started several years ago when he was in 3eme

(the equivalent of 10th grade) in Port-au-Prince, where he had moved to attend high school. A classmate borrowed one of his notebooks. Simon believes that he became ill as soon as she gave it back to him. He claims that his notebook had been tampered with, that someone who wished him ill had put a *wanga* (magic) after him. He could not get better. He stopped attending school and went back to his village. His mother took him to see a *bòkò* (witch doctor), who performed services for him, prepared medicines and baths, and called the *lwa*. But Simon said he "did not believe in these things. Sometimes *vodou* is not bad; some of it is good. Some people profit by it, make money". Since his

> uncles have money, even though they were pastors, they paid for the services. They would try everything so I would not die. My mother is the only one of her siblings who has not converted. She believes that if her child is sick, she should try everything. She does not practice *vodou*, but my sister does, she has a spirit who dances in her head".

The *bòkò* did not help his illness; Simon broke the medicine. Later on his uncles paid for him to come to Miami aboard a *kantè*.

Augustin's story, on the other hand, illustrated the fact that while some of the immigrants resisted conversion, they also realized that practicing *vodou* was not socially acceptable in this country. Augustin had not been to church for a few weeks, so I asked him why. He said that he did not go because he was having "*vent fè mal*" (tummy ache). I asked if he had also missed work, and he said no, that he only felt bad on Sundays. I commented that he seemed to have a strange illness, and he answered: "anyway they want to baptize me and I don't want to be baptized." I then asked him if he was a vodouist and he said "no, I am not mixed up with that kind of thing." Later on in the conversation however, he told me of his family's cult house, his ancestral gods, and religious experiences.

Immigrants claim that Protestant churches in America were more sympathetic than Catholics to the plight of Haitian boat people. Simone agreed that there were fewer Catholics among the Haitians in Rochester. She added that several of the immigrants liked "*legliz ki cho*" (animated services) because they reminded them of *vodou* services.

Converting to Protestantism is a form of *demele*. It is both a social move toward the center, and an edge against misfortune. In America, Haitian immigrants perceive that being Christian is more acceptable than being vodouist. Some take on attributes which they feel will work to their advantage, while at the same time "serving the *lwa*," in case *levangil* should fail them.

From Creole-French to Creole-English, making it in the United States

Aside from religion, literacy and linguistic proficiency are among the most important status markers in Haitian social structure. A great deal of internal migration in Haiti is organized around providing an education for one's children. There are few elementary and no secondary schools in the rural areas. Haitians perceive that learning French is the first step out of the cycle of poverty and dependency that illiteracy creates. They believe that it is a tool that will enable them to cross social, as well as economic boundaries. *"Rout edikasyon se rout sove"* (education is the way to escape), said an informant.

Education is an investment for the entire family. As one member is able to progress, he/she in turn will "pull" others. In rural areas and among urban poor, the entire extended family is involved in *demele* to provide some of its members with the opportunity to go to school and learn French. These strategies often involve relocation of certain family members to an urban area, and even emigration.

Most of the Haitian immigrants living in Rochester had a history of internal migration in Haiti. As they settled in America, they sought to use the same Haitian strategies, adapting them to fit their new situation in America. Some moved to an urban area in order to improve their chances "for a better life" for themselves and especially their children. Andre was eager to stay in Rochester to learn English and get a good job. He wanted to be settled before sending for his daughter, and later, his sons. He said that the agricultural communities in Florida did not offer the same educational opportunities as the city did, and that to bring his children there would not be profitable. He was willing to "*sakrifye kò mwen*" (sacrifice myself) so that his children would get a break.

Most of the immigrants made a connection between the need to learn to speak English and finding a job.

People who work with Haitian immigrants observe that in some cases, however, their short range strategies did not allow them to plan adequately for the future. Mr. Larosilliere from Catholic Charities, himself a Haitian, pointed out that immigrants would often drop out of educational programs, once established in a job. They seemed to be satisfied with their situation, and lacked the motivation to pursue their studies beyond learning to speak the language. He suggested that the immigrants did not always recognize the link between better education and better-paying jobs. I propose that for Haitians who are illiterate, learning to speak English is a difficult task, and learning to read and write in English is overwhelming. I suggest that one possible solution would be to teach them to read and write in Creole, at least in the initial phases. However, Mr. Larosilliere thought that Haitian attitudes regarding the relationship between French and education might work against it. An education in Creole does not carry as much social value as an education in French. One could argue that Mr. Larosilliere and the anthropologist both bring to this discussion Haitian values in proposing solutions.

French is certainly a marker of higher social
status (Classes I and II), and knowing this study's
population, I avoided initiating conversations in
French. During my fieldwork, I only held one conversation in French, with Jacques. Even though I was
aware that a few others could speak French, it was
never used between other immigrants and myself, nor
among the immigrants themselves. Simone said that
those "who know French are uncomfortable using it because they feel that they don't speak well and will be
criticized." She added that "few use French here.
Those who can are respected for their education, their
knowledge. Several Haitians here do not have any
education."

It can be argued that the immigrants and I made an
attempt to create Haitian unity and to avoid that
which separates Haitians. Even though Simone was
well-educated (she had completed her Baccalaureate),
she never spoke to me in French. Instead, she would
code-switch or use a formal urban Creole. She told me
that she never spoke French at home, that although she
knew it, she did not use it. She only spoke French
when she was in school in Haiti. She thought that
French was just a social marker, and that Creole was

more important to Haitians; "it is the language of the people, and not all can afford enough education to speak French." Jacques, on the other hand, had a very different outlook. "If you speak French very well in Haiti, you can gain access to all places." His attitude toward French extended toward other languages as well; "if you learn English, Spanish,.. you can go everywhere". Jacques expressed the belief that "education is the way to success, to better jobs anywhere." Their individual attitudes were reflected in the way they approached life in America. Simone avoided learning English, remained within her small network of Haitian friends and had problems adapting to life in Rochester. Jacques learned English and went on to obtain a high school diploma. He was able to move into better-paying and higher status jobs. He was also able to function outside the Haitian community and even to act as mediator for other Haitians.

Cultural ideas that Haitians have about education, and the social meaning of French in Haiti, influence their strategies of adaptation in Rochester. Haitian immigrants perceive French to be associated with a hierarchical class structure and to have a divisive influence in Haitian society. On the other hand, they perceive that English has a unifying function within the American social system, and that upward mobility is not predicated by the social meaning of English. Knowledge of English becomes for them a way to achieve social and economic advancement outside of the Haitian class system. Social cleavages within the community are also being redefined. One's ability and willingness to accept French as a social marker is being replaced by proficiency in English, and subsequent economic gains (see Buchanan 1979, 1983). *Demele* in the form of "working hard, and making the best of situations," is not enough to move from periphery to center in the urban context - it also includes a good command of English and a commitment to higher education.

ROCHESTER HAITIAN COMMUNITY IN 1986

By the end of 1986, important changes had taken place within the Rochester Haitian community. The most important change was that the rate of employment within the community was over 90%, and several immigrants held more than one job. At least two families were reunited, as immigrants were successful in "pulling" more relatives to this country.   Three babies were born;   two immigrants were granted residence permits.   Most of those who remained in Rochester had settled down to   new routines.   They still attended church services, and several drove their own cars. For most, the risks had paid off.   An informant had analyzed his decision to move to Rochester in the following terms:

> It's like spending money to buy a goat.
> With luck she will have kids and you can
> realize a profit. On the other hand,
> she may die before getting pregnant, in
> which case you lost your investment.

Several problems remained.   There were still very few families in the city, and the immigrants perceived this as their most pressing concern.   They complained of loneliness.   The men decried the fact that there were no available Haitian women in the city.   The ratio of men to women in Rochester is less than 3:1. With the exception of a single older woman, all the other women had Haitian partners.   The women came to the city to meet their spouses, and most of them had been married before their husbands left Haiti. Several immigrants were dating white women, others formed relationships with blacks.   There have been several marriages between Haitian men and American

women. I attended the wedding of Fritz to a Black
American woman. Some of these unions were *mariaj biznis* (business marriage), arranged for the explicit
purpose of obtaining permanent residence status.

The lack of communication between the urban groups
of immigrants remained a problem. Social differences,
real and perceived, affected the development of a community. Cleavages based on the distinction between
urban and rural Haitians were maintained. Further
divisions between *moun sòt* and *moun eklere*, made on
the basis of education and knowledge of English, were
evident. At the same time, Haitian immigrants in
Rochester emphasized their wish to become part of
American society. It is possible that this wish stood
in the way of creating a Haitian community. For them,
being part of American society meant economic and social advancement within the larger context of the
American system. It is moving to the center. Their
center had shifted from "making it" in a Haitian environment, to making it in an American context.
Demele strategies included searching outside the
Haitian community for ways of "making it" better in
the larger society.

In 1984, the Geneseo Migrant Center invited former migrant workers, living in Rochester, to attend All Camp Day programs and other cultural events that the Center offered, and only a few participated. But when they were asked, at the beginning of 1986, to cooperate with the Center in an educational program for migrant workers in Wyoming County, the response was positive.

The program is designed to teach ESL to migrant workers during the season, and requires the active participation of the former migrants. They were directly involved in drafting a grant proposal and took part in an interview with a local agency interested in funding self-development programs. If funded, this program would provide a link between urban and migrant populations. The urban immigrants would participate in designing, implementing, and assessing the instructional program. They were eager to serve as role models for Haitians still in the migrant stream. The urban residents saw themselves as being *patron* to the migrant workers. They wrote that their participation would "illustrate by example to the workers the possibilities for development in this

country through the acquisition of the English language." By setting themselves in this role, they are
re-establishing a Haitian hierarchy. They become
patron to migrant clients and serve as examples of
successful *demele*.

There were several problems with "making it" for
the rural immigrants. Even though they made economic
gains, their lack of understanding of American culture
limited their progress. Their standard of living did
improve, but they said that life, in general, was not
better. Their social universe was very limited: there
were no kin, and the friendship networks available to
them were very limited. In the absence of traditional
patterns of mutual help, they relied on social service
agencies for legal advice, and for resolving social
and cultural problems. The Rochester population made
more use of support services than the rural population. The migrant workers were in a confined environment where most decisions were made for them, and in a
community where everyone did the same thing. The urban immigrants were socially isolated. They had to
struggle for survival, make decisions, and deal with
new problems without the support of their traditional
system. Whereas migrant workers did not need to know

English to function in the migrant system, success in the urban milieu depended a great deal on one's proficiency in that language.

The concept of community, as a group working together for the benefit of all its members, is not a Haitian concept. Francis observed that, in Philadelphia:

> the idea of working as a group does not appear.. to be constructive for these Haitians...Getting and disseminating information, obtaining jobs, and favors are done through informal networks consisting primarily of family and trusted friends (1984:12).

Instead, Haitians organize their social space and their relationships around the extended family (*fanmi*), and informal networks (*moun pa*: one of mine), whose ties may extend across class lines. Haitian immigrants in Rochester were re-creating these familiar structures. They infused their relations with social and service agencies and churches with the spirit of kinship amity. They extended to these organizations the same feelings of love, as well as moral rights, duties, and obligations, that characterize real kinship relations.

Haitian cultural ideas regarding hierarchical class structure based on the oppositions of rural-urban, *moun sòt-moun eklere*, influenced the adaptation process and the organization of the urban community. Even though the Haitian community of Rochester is small and relatively homogeneous, it shared many similarities with larger urban Haitian communities in the United States, such as the ones of New York City, Boston, and Philadelphia.[26]

CHAPTER VII

CONCLUSION

The main concern of this study has been the migration and adaptation processes of Haitian boat people in the United States. It focuses on the description and analysis of these processes among a rural and an urban group of Haitian immigrants, in two different settings, (a rural environment and a city). The study shows that cultural ideas that Haitians have guide their strategies and inform the choices they make.

In the following, I summarize some of the key findings presented in the previous chapters, and in particular the implications that these have for American public policy vis à vis Haitian immigrants. I argue for the importance of understanding the natives' views, i.e. Haitian immigrants' cultural ideas and social aspirations.

In Chapter I, I place this study in the context of previous anthropological studies on migration and adaptation of Haitian boat people. I argued that *demele* is the ethos that informs Haitians' choices and decisions, and permeates the strategies that Haitians use. The concept of periphery was introduced to describe the social position that Haitians wish to leave, and the concept of center, the place in society that they aspire to occupy. I argue that, facing American society, all Haitian immigrants see themselves as a *nasyon*, different from other *nasyon*. In social interaction among Haitians, immigrants recognize social differences; urban immigrants see themselves as *moun eklere*, and refer to rural immigrants as *moun sòt*. It is shown that these distinctions, which are based on Haitian cultural ideas regarding the hierarchical nature of Haitian society, are replicated in the communities they create in the United States.

In Chapter II, I demonstrate the importance of understanding the historical and ecological context in which Haitian contemporary *conscience collective* was formed. I argue that several issues, such as migration and adaptation, are better understood when placed in this context. I show that Haitians' successful fight for freedom is not only an important component in their present *conscience collective*, it also guides their social relation with Black Americans. Haitians boat people's reluctance to associate with Black Americans is rooted in their own freedom. I also argue that the historical perspective sheds light on the causes of Haitian migration. This chapter demonstrates that migration of Haitians of rural and urban poor origins, is caused, in part, by social, demographic, economic, and political factors that have their roots in Haiti's history.

Chapter III offers an overview of Haitian migration. I show that the presence of Haitian illegal immigrants has often been considered a social problem in the host communities. As early as the 1920's, the Cuban and Dominican governments tried to stem the flow of Haitian seasonal labor in their countries. More recently, in the 70's, the Bahamians became alarmed at the size of their Haitian community (23% of the total Bahamian population, Marshall 1979), and adopted strong extradition and interception measures to contain the rate of Haitian immigration. Illegal immigration of Haitians to the United States was thus a logical outcome of a long process. As the migrants were no longer welcomed in the Caribbean Basin, the southern coast of Florida became, for them, the next available port.

The illegal immigration of Haitian boat people into the United States was the theme of Chapter IV. For the first time in the history of Haitian illegal

immigration, the problem is given serious consideration in the United States. It is shown that Haitian
immigration has social and economic effects on the
home and the host societies. While Haitian immigrants
talk about lack of economic opportunities and political repression in Haiti as the reasons for emigration,
this study identifies other "push" factors, such as
demographic pressure, and the hierarchical social
structure of Haitian society. It also shows that perceived economic and social opportunities attract
Haitian immigrants to the United States. I suggest
that recent political events in Haiti will not significantly affect the rate of migration of Haitians of
rural and urban poor origins. As long as "push" factors, such as demographic pressure, economic and social barriers remain, Haitians will have to look elsewhere for a way to "make it".

This study presents Haitian immigrants as actors
who take advantage of opportunities. Among rural
Haitians, the decision to migrate is sometimes taken
in the context of the extended family. I argue that
migrants, as members of these extended families, act
on behalf of, and for, their kin, as well as for themselves.

Migration, it is shown here, is a two-way process. Immigrants have to adapt to a new culture and society, and the host communities have to absorb immigrants of different cultural backgrounds.   Illegal immigration also raises moral and legal issues for the host society, at the national and the local level.   It raises questions such as: Should all immigrants be allowed to remain in the United States?   How far should state and local governments go in supporting the basic needs of illegal aliens?   What are the legal and civil rights of such persons?   Facing these and other questions inevitably brings about changes in the legal system, as well as in other social spheres.

The adaptation process of Haitian boat people was the topic of Chapters V and VI.   The study demonstrates that, in America, Haitian immigrants tend to maintain the rural-urban distinctions that exist in Haiti, that Haitians of rural origins tend to settle in agricultural communities, and that immigrants of urban origins often move into urban areas.

Chapter V focuses on Haitian immigrants in the migrant labor system.   The study shows that relations between rural Haitian men and women undergo a change in America.   Women lose their productive independence,

as well as the prestige that accompanies their
reproductive activity. They no longer have the
economic freedom and the ability to leave unions that
are no longer satisfactory. At the same time, mother-
hood loses some of its traditional meanings.

Chapters V and VI show that among Haitians, black
and white color categories do not necessarily reflect
racial ascription. Rather, they serve to identify social categories. In this context, black is associated
with rural and low class, and white with urban and upper class. Rural immigrants refer to authority
figures as *blan*, white. They describe peasants as
nwa, black, and associate poverty and blackness with
agricultural labor. As people move up the social
hierarchy, they become, in the eyes of Haitians, more
"white". A Haitian proverb illustrates this claim:
"*nèg rich se mulat, mulat pòv se nèg.*" (a rich black
is a mulatto, a poor mulatto is a black.) These observations point to the fact that an analytic distinction can be made between the way Haitians arrange
their world at the structural level, and the way they
perceive their world at the ideational level. Color
hierarchy is associated with class hierarchy, and is
more a social issue than a cultural one.

Chapter V also shows that during the process of adaptation, Haitians of rural origins rely mainly on "group-oriented" strategies predicated on kinship amity and kinship ties. Their center remains anchored in Haiti, and they maintain kinship rights, duties, and obligations vis à vis their extended families.

Chapter VI demonstrates that, although urban immigrants appear to use "individualistic" strategies, this is not always the case. Urban immigrants draw extensively on resources available in the host community, such as resettlement, social, and legal agencies, and churches. They infuse their relations with these formal organizations with the spirit of kinship amity. The organizations become incorporated as fictive kin, and the same rules of conduct are applied to them. Urban immigrants often refer to agencies as "my family", and "my heart". These affective terms, in fact, imply social obligations on both sides. The immigrants are grateful to the agencies, and feel that they owe them allegiance. On the other hand, they expect the agencies to provide help and support. Those who work with Haitian immigrants and formulate policies should be aware of the importance of fictive kin ties for Haitian immigrants. It might help create a better understanding of their needs, as well as their actions.

Chapter VI shows that Haitians in Rochester are reluctant to form a community. I suggest that urban immigrants are willing to sacrifice community cohesiveness in favor of adaptation to American society. They realize that the larger society has a negative image of Haitians; therefore they try to de-emphasize their Haitian identity. At the same time, Class III immigrants perceive that by dissociating themselves from those they consider as *moun sòt*, they will be freer to acquire the markers of their aspired center.

Several issues, such as the full meaning of *demele*, gender relations among the urban population, and the problems that illegal immigration create for the host society, should be further investigated. In this study, I chose to emphasize the immigrants' point of view, their cultural ideas, their social aspira-tions, and the meaning that America has for them.

POSTSCRIPT

Many changes have taken place since the research was first written as a dissertation. Although there has been a change of government in Haiti and a new immigration bill in the U.S., the adaptation process continues for the boat people.

The most dramatic development in Haiti was the overthrow of the Duvalier regime, on February 7, 1986, following a popular uprising. This uprising was also significant because, for the first time in Haiti's history, religious leaders and citizens from all walks of life and class backgrounds were united for the same purpose. This event, dubbed Haiti's "second Independence", signaled the end of an era of political repression, and violation of human and civil rights. After nearly thirty years of tyranny, there is finally the promise of a democratic future. The political machinery is being reactivated; there is a new provisional government, parties and labor unions are being formed, elections are planned, public debate is allowed, and freedom of the press has been reinstated.

As part of this new beginning, Haitians voted overwhelmingly for a new constitution on the 29th of March. This constitution contains measures designed to safeguard basic civil rights, decentralize power, and introduce socio-economic reforms. It recognizes French and Creole as official languages, all forms of worship (although the constitution does not mention *vodou* explicitly, its inclusion is strongly implied), and the need for land reform.

On the surface these political changes seem to indicate a trend toward the improvement of social and economic conditions and, subsequently, a decrease in Haitian emigration. In reality, Haiti is suffering from long-term neglect: the economic situation is very precarious, political unrest persists more than a year after the overthrow of Duvalier, and emigration continues.

Exports have fallen, foreign investors are waiting for a more stable government, and tourism is at an all-time low. There are as yet no new sources of employment for the urban poor and no alleviation of the economic situation in rural areas. On the

political front, there is a proliferation of can-
didates and political parties, but no clear direction. According to some Haitians, those now in
power had ties with the Duvalier regime and nothing
has changed. The country is plagued by major
strikes, and the people demand an impartial government and less international intervention in Haiti's
internal affairs.

It appears, then, that the factors that fueled
the boat people migration are still relevant in
Haiti now. Thus I do not foresee a change in the
migration pattern of Haitians of urban poor and
rural origins in the near future. Informants report
that *kannté* are still leaving from Haiti and that
boat people are still coming in. As long as Haiti's
economy is poor, demographic pressures are high,
farming conditions remain primitive, and social and
cultural divisions are still rigidly maintained, un-
derprivileged Haitians have to go elsewhere to make
a living. It will take time to reverse the trend
and to mend the rifts even after the political
situation is stable again. Economic opportunities
and social conditions at home will have to coun-
teract the "pulls" from abroad.

In the United States, after several years of debate, Congress passed the Immigration Reform and Control Act (IRCA) of 1986. This new law makes it possible for illegal and undocumented aliens who have entered the United States on or before January 1, 1982, to legalize their status. This law also contains special provisions for Cuban and Haitian entrants and for agricultural workers.

Although many Haitians will benefit from IRCA, several may be excluded because they lack documents proving identity and length of stay in the U.S., are unable to pay the heavy processing fees required by INS, or are just afraid to trust the system. Those who do not qualify for legalization will have to decide between returning home, moving to some other country, or continue to live as illegal aliens in the U.S..

The Haitian community of Rochester continues to grow and prosper. The original core group is now well-established, the employment rate continues to be high, and the immigrants are adjusting to life in the city. Some have bought homes, others have started businesses and families. There is still no organized Haitian community, but several networks have been developed. The Rochester community has also had its casualties; one man was deported, and the fate of his family is uncertain at this time. His American-born children have the right to remain in this country, but their illegal alien parents cannot be here with them.

The picture is quite different for Haitian boat people living in agricultural communities in Florida. The mechanization of potato farming in the Genesee Valley changed the labor needs of farmers, and Haitians have lost a steady source of employment. A crew leader who used to bring three hundred men to Livingston County only has a crew of fourteen this year. Haitians farmworkers are trying other crops. Those with good skills can pick apples, cucumbers, and tomatoes. More Haitians are also forming their own crews. Fewer Haitians are expected this year; on one hand employers are weary of hiring aliens because of the strict penalties included in IRCA; on the other, immigrants who have started the legalization process in Florida feel that they should remain there to continue the

process. Others do not fully understand the implications and the various provisions of the new law
and fear being sent back to Haiti.

High rate of unemployment, housing, health, and
other social problems continue to plague Haitians
living in agricultural communities, especially in
Florida.   These communities are becoming isolated
ethnic enclaves whose inhabitants have little access
to mainstream America.   Like marginal people
everywhere, while trying to make it, they often use
strategies considered beyond the boundaries of acceptable behavior. For example, Haitians in Florida
are entering the drug business, dealing in crack,
and recently some migrant workers have been arrested
in upstate New York. When I talked about these ar-
rests with my informants last fall, they commented
that Haitians do not do drugs because they have no
money to spare. The dealers are just "*moun sót*",
trying to make "a quick buck" by taking advantage of
weak individuals. I have learned that upon achieving their stated goals - enough money to start a
business and move out of the ghetto, for example -
dealers will then resume a normal life. This
problem is a cause of concern for those who work

with boat people - it casts a shadow on the whole community.

The changes described above are indeed very important. They serve to underline the fact that the social, economic, and cultural factors that prompted the boat people migration and influenced their adaptation in the United States continue to be relevant.

Demele strategies and the desire to move from periphery to center need to be fully investigated. Little attention is paid to Haitians living in secluded agricultural communities. I feel that more studies of this group are important for understanding the adaptation process of populations of rural origins in the United States as well as Haitian culture and social organization. There is also a need for more research to provide data that could be used to develop programs that would offer positive alternatives to help Haitians overcome yet more problems.

"Deyè mòn, gen mòn".

"Behind every mountain there is another mountain"

APPENDIX I

IMMIGRATION STATUS

The major obstacle to adaptation for Haitian boat people has been the uncertainty of their legal status. Prior to the enactment of the 1987 Immigration Reform Act, in the eyes of the INS, Haitian boat people were neither political refugees, legal immigrants, nor illegal aliens. Few qualified for political asylum - the majority were considered to be economic refugees. The Haitians felt that the distinction was hard to make and that in Haiti, economic conditions and political repression often go hand in hand. They claimed that while poverty is extreme and pervasive, "the Haitian Government does virtually nothing to improve the general welfare of the masses but rather exploits and exacerbates existing conditions; and repression is pervasive and triggered by the slightest imagined opposition" (Stepick 1983:178).

Until 1980, all Haitian immigrants caught while entering the country illegally were either denied asylum and placed in exclusion proceedings, or arbitrarily deported. In July, 1980, a historic decision handed down by Judge King of the Southern District Court of Florida ordered the INS to halt deportation of Haitians. Judge King maintained that the INS' treatment of the Haitians had been motivated, to some degree, by racial prejudice, and that "over the past 17 years, Haitian claims for asylum and refuge have been systematically denied, while all others have been granted" (Stepick 1983: 186). This court decision coincided with the Mariel sealift of Cuban refugees and a substantial increase in Haitian illegal immigration. At the same time, President Carter introduced the Refugee Act of 1980, designed to eliminate bias in favor of those fleeing Communist countries and against those fleeing countries such as Haiti. In spite of this official stand, Cubans were quickly processed, classified as asylum applicants, and released, while Haitians were classified as illegal aliens and put in exclusion proceedings. The media and the public protested this unfair treatment that denied refugee status to

Haitian immigrants, for allegedly being no more than economic refugees, while at the same time welcoming Cubans for the same reasons. In response to these pressures, President Carter announced the administration's new Cuban-Haitian Entrants program in May of 1980. Under this new program, Cuban and Haitian individuals who entered the United States illegally before October 1980, could present themselves to the INS and receive an INS form I-94 stamped "status pending", and be granted indefinite parole, as well as the right to work, receive social assistance, and health services. It is estimated that about 40,000 Haitian immigrants received I-94's between April 10, 1980 and October 10, 1980. Anyone arriving after October 1980 was detained and issued an unstamped I-94 that granted limited, renewable parole, work authorization, and some assistance. Members of both groups could be called to undergo exclusion hearings at any time, were not able to sponsor relatives in this country, and could not legally reenter the U.S.

In October 1981, the Reagan administration tightened the reins against the Haitian refugees by ordering the Coast Guard to intercept boats suspected of transporting Haitians to the United States and to tow such boats back to Haiti. Under this system, refugees' claims were adjudicated outside of U.S. territory (thus outside of the jurisdiction of the INS), in an area where the provisions of the Immigration and Nationality Act and the Refugee Act of 1980 did not apply. As a result, the flow of Haitians dropped significantly. Stepick (1983) reports that fewer than 120 Haitians arrived between January and October of 1982, as compared with nearly 8,000 for the same period in 1981. Those undocumented aliens already in the U.S. and all unintercepted new arrivals were to be detained until their legal status was resolved. Haitians were presented with the choice of remaining in detention indefinitely, or returning to Haiti where, many claimed, they would be persecuted. After intensive lobbying, protests, letter-writing campaigns by various civil groups and members of Haitian communities in the U.S., hunger strikes by the inmates, and the intervention of the Organization of American States, Judge Spellman of the United States District Court for the Southern District of Florida ordered the release of about 1,900 Haitians held in federal detention centers.   This group of immigrants is referred to as "Spellman cases".   Fearing that the ruling would encourage more Haitians to enter the country illegally,   Judge Spellman ruled that Haitians arriving after the date of the court order would be detained indefinitely.   In April 1983, about 200 Haitians were being held in Krome and 10 in Brooklyn's Naval Yard, while 75 had voluntarily returned to Haiti.   In April 27, 1984, there were still 228 Haitians in Krome North.   Inmates were released in care of sponsors or for humanitarian reasons.

At the same time, several cases were up for debate in different courts.   A Supreme Court decision is expected on a case heard in March 1985 regarding "the constitutional right for equal protection for all races and nationalities" (HCC Newsletter 1985:4), and especially the "right of excludable Haitian refugees to challenge the discriminatory practices of the INS" (idem).   As Stepick (1983) notes, the courts have been the legal battleground for the Haitian refugee dispute, a forum where the views of the INS, the Administration, and the refugees are heard.

However, the issue could not be resolved only by
the courts - appropriate legislative action and
guidelines were necessary to clarify the existing
discrepancy between legal principles and administrative practices (See Congressional Quarterly 1980,
1984; Dept. of Health and Human Services Memorandum
1983; HCC Newsletter 1985; Stepick 1983, 1984b).
Congress was also considering "a multifaceted bill
to revamp the nation's immigration laws"
(Congressional Quarterly 1984: 1493). The first bill
was introduced in 1981, in 1982 Senator Simpson and
Congressman Mazzoli, Chairmen of the Senate and
House Immigration Subcommittees, sponsored their own
bill, but final approval was not reached that year.
This bill, together with companion bills sponsored
by Congressmen Rodino and Roybal, were presented
each year to Congress. In 1986, the 99th Congress
passed the Immigration Reform and Control Act which,
they claim, should satisfy all interest groups.
Four provisions of this bill are of special interest
to undocumented and out of status Haitian alien
residents: the Haitian-Cuban adjustment provisions,
the general legalization provisions for undocumented
aliens, legalization for special agricultural

workers, and the registry for those who have lived
continuously in the U.S. since 1972 in an unlawful
status (National Coalition for Haitian Refugees,
Fact Sheet #1, 1987).   Applicants should be able to
demonstrate that they have continuously resided in
the U.S. since before January 1, 1982.   Affected
aliens have to apply for status adjustment within
two years after enactment of this law (H.R.23, Jan.
8, 1985).   Those Haitians who do not qualify for
legalization will undergo deportation hearings and
sent back to Haiti.

APPENDIX II

RESETTLEMENT AGENCIES

Several agencies are involved in refugee and immigrant resettlement programs. Local and State
government agencies have assistance programs such as
rent subsidies, food stamps, and job training
programs; they also sponsor social programs run by
refugee and immigrant community centers. These
public agencies also fund private organizations
whose purpose is to facilitate the resettlement
process and provide a variety of programs geared at
helping new immigrants and refugees become self-
sufficient. I had the opportunity to meet a number
of people in several agencies and to become familiar
with their services. I describe in more detail
below a few that were of particular interest to the
population that I studied.

o The Catholic Family Center of Rochester has
been involved with the Haitian immigrants since
1980. They offer a variety of services that fall
into two broad categories; resettlement and assistance programs.

Resettlement programs sponsor new immigrants in the community, help them find housing and proper health care, and enroll them in schools and ESL programs. These are short term assistance programs funded by the national office of the U.S. Catholic Conference. In addition, the Rochester area is one of seven sites in the U.S. that offers resettlement services to Haitian immigrants living in the Miami area through an outreach program designed to help those who cannot find permanent employment. The Center has sponsored 24 Haitians between January 1984 and April 1985. People at the Center feel that the program is successful and they attribute its high rate of success to the efficiency of their social workers and to the determination of the immigrants themselves.

Assistance programs offer long term services like job development and social adjustment programs, translation and counseling services.

The Catholic Center is also a member of the Rochester Interfaith Council on Immigrants and Refugees (RICUR) and coordinates legal assistance

programs for Haitians undergoing exclusion or deportation hearings.   RICUR is now coordinating the implementation of the new immigration law for the
Rochester area.

   o Legal Assistance Program.   Since the Fall of
1982, several volunteer attorneys from Rochester
have assumed the defense of Haitian parolees seeking
asylum in the United States.   Eighteen Haitian immigrants, all Spellman cases, are currently undergoing exclusion or deportation hearings in Rochester.
Their cases are being debated before an Administrative Court presided by an INS judge.   No action has
been taken by the court on the cases that were heard
in the Fall of 1984 and Spring of 1985.   Should they
be found excludable, their cases will go to a District Court under the Federal Court system.   At this
point their chances of obtaining asylum are bleak -
the Administrative Court system follows administration policies - and at this time the administration
is still undecided in its position toward "illegal
and undocumented aliens".

   o The Parsells Avenue Community Church has maintained a high degree of involvement with its Haitian
members and the Haitian community at large.   The

church has sponsored several individuals, organized special worship services for its Haitian parishioners, provided educational and counseling services, and has helped in the development of self-help community programs. It is interested in helping the Haitian immigrants living in Rochester to form a united and self-sufficient community. Its pastor has been personally involved in lobbying for the passage and implementation of the Immigration Reform and Control Act of 1986. He has also taken part in the defense of the parolees both as an expert witness and as a consultant.

o Farmworker Legal Services provides legal services to migrants in civil cases: work and wage problems, immigration problems, cases involving worker compensation and occupational hazards. Although this organization focuses mainly on the migrant farm worker population, it also maintains contact with former migrants who have resettled in the city and channels specific problems to the proper agencies.

o Rural Opportunities Inc. is an agency providing support services for migrant farm workers and resettlement assistance to former migrants moving into urban areas. Usually these services are handled by field offices located in farming communities in several states on the East coast - the Central Office for the Northeast Region is in Rochester. The Rochester office became involved with the Haitians in 1982 when a group of ten workers decided to resettle in the city. It also arranges for educational services to Haitian migrant workers in several counties. Rural Opportunities is primarily funded by the U.S. Department of Labor; its Haitian resettlement program was part of a Cuban-Haitian Entrants program financed by a special grant from the New York State Department of Social Services.

o The Community Bible Church of Rochester has also sponsored, counseled, and helped several Haitian immigrants. They graciously lent me space for group meetings and individual interviews.

NOTES

1. *Conscience collective* is used here in the strict sense of Durkheim's definition as the "collective and common conscience... (which) connects successive generations with one another. It is, thus, an entirely different thing from particular consciences, although it can be realized only through them" (Durkheim 1933: 80). See also Robert Alun Jones (1986) on Durkheim.

2. I am aware of and familiar with the literature on immigration in the U.S.. I chose not to address this issue in the present study, but to emphasize Haitian immigration to the United States. I am also aware that some of the characteristics displayed by Haitian immigrants have been noted for other immigrant groups. I leave the comparative aspect of this problem for later studies.

3. For a review of the literature on migration, see Graves and Graves 1974.

4. See also Fjellman and Gladwin 1985, and Laguerre 1978 on the role of the Haitian extended family in formulating strategies of migration.

5. See also Woldemikael 1985, Vincent 1978, Philpott 1968 and 1970, Graves and Graves 1974, Laguerre 1978, 1984 on strategies.

6. What Schneider (1980) refers to as "diffuse and enduring solidarity", and Fortes (1969) as "kinship amity" are essentially the same. Both authors talk about moral obligations. Although Schneider himself sees a difference, I follow Craig (1979) in seeing a similarity.

7. Haitians refer to their religion as *sèvi lwa*, "serving the gods".

8. See Levi-Strauss (1963) on categories of oppositions. I use his terms as analytical concepts.

9. I sometimes refer to Classes I and II as upper classes, and Classes III and IV as lower classes. What some authors define as *classe moyenne* (middle class) is here included as Class III.

10. Clearances were obtained from all informants at time of interviews. However, the names of all informants, as well as names of camps, are fictional.
    The Haitian Creole orthography used throughout this study is based on the system proposed by the Creole Institute of the University of Indiana.

11. I have been visiting migrant camps in Livingston and Wyoming Counties since 1983. In 1985, the largest employer in Livingston County mechanized his operations. Subsequently, the number of Haitians in the area decreased. Instead, more Haitians went to work in apple orchards along the southern shores of Lake Ontario. I followed them and have been working with them in Orleans and Wayne Counties.

12. In-depth interviews were conducted over several sessions.

13. Several Haitian boat people will qualify for permanent resident status under the new Immigration and Reform Act of 1986 (see Appendix I).

14. According to Haitian etiquette, a married woman is often addressed as *Madame*, in French, or *Madanm* in Creole, followed by the first name of her husband.

15. Several authors discuss the role of *marronage* in slave revolts; see Davis, H. 1967, Genovese 1979, Leyburn 1941, Metraux 1937, Rainsford 1805.

16. One of the outcomes of the American Occupation was a revival of traditional art, literature, and music in Haiti. The renaissance of patriotism also fostered the formation of

rebel groups called *cacos* composed of a cross-section of the population united to fight the invasion.

17. According to the *Noiriste* thesis, color and class issues are one and the same. *Noiristes* claim that the history of Haiti reflects the struggle between a mulatto elite and the black masses, and that color prejudice, on the part of the mulattoes, has been responsible for Haiti's social problems since colonial times. *Noirisme* is related to *negritude* ideology which implies that "the Black man is a man endowed with a particular human nature" (Nicholls 1985: 48). For more detailed discussions and analyses, see Nicholls (1979, 1985), Davis (1967), Labelle (1978).

   More conservative proponents of *negritude* in Haiti insist that class conflict has always been a more complicated matter than one of color.

18. According to the new Constitution, Catholicism is no longer the official state religion; it recognizes all forms of worship.

19. For more information on diglossia, code-switching, and gallicizing, see Valdman (1968, 1975, 1983, 1984); Scotton (1980); Bentolila (1978); Stewart (1968); and Ferguson (1964).

20. I owe the distinction between culture and social structure to Fortes (1969). I also draw on this work for a better understanding of social liminality. His work is also useful in making a distinction between analysis and description (1970).

21. Allman and Richman (1985) note that the word *kannte*, used to mean transport, "was appropriated from the brand name of the Japanese motor, Canter, which powers the fast, brightly decorated Haitian trucks. Since the period of boat migrations, the term has been used to refer ironically to the pitifully small sailboats on which peasants attempted the voyage to Miami." Boat people are often referred to as *moun kannte, kannte* people.

22. This is no longer true. INS regulations regarding the rights of parents of children born in America to remain in this country with them have changed.

23. Jacques is one of the most successful boat people in Rochester. He has learned to drive and has bought a car; he has also saved enough money to buy a house. He rents out rooms to help pay his mortgage.

24. See Carole Stack (1974) on reciprocity as "strategy for survival" among low-income urban blacks.

25. See work of Labelle (1978) on the relationship between color and social class.

26. Other writers have noticed the same urban:rural opposition. Francis (1984) reports that "these social and ideological distinctions" are also found in Philadephia. Fontaine (1976: 119), commenting on the hierarchical structure of the Haitian community of Boston, says that it "is much less blatantly stratified than that of New York. This has a great deal to do with the smaller size of the Boston Haitian population". Buchanan (1983: 8) writes that "Haitians tend to view the New York City immigrant 'community' primarily in terms of sociocultural divisions which existed in Haiti".

GLOSSARY

bòkò: *vodou* priest.

bòt: boat, usually a motor boat.

Bouki ak Malis: uncle and nephew duo of Haitian folktales. Malis is clever and full of tricks, while Bouki is slow witted and gullible.

chèf: boss, leader, someone in authority, for example *chef lakou*, *chef seksyon* (sheriff).

demanbre: symbolic center of a *lakou*, *vodou* shrine associated with ancestors and family *lwa*.

demele: to make ends meet; to manage in the face of hardship; to find a solution; hustle and bustle. Synonym of *degaje*.

doktè fey: herb doctor, well versed in the healing qualities of plants.

hougan (ougan): a *vodou* leader, a dynamic power within his community. Teacher, healer, he serves the as a link between his followers and the world of the spirits.

kay: peasant house, usually having mud walls and a thatched roof.

konbit: cooperative work party in which land owners provide food, drink, and music in return for help from their neighbors, usually a reciprocal arrangement. *Konbit* can be held to plant a field, harvest crops, build a house, a road, etc.

konesans: acquired knowledge; awareness.

lakou: a family compound; a social group usually composed of kinsmen who live together on family land. Members of a *lakou* share access to economic resources, responsabilities for mutual aid, and ritual obligations to ancestors. People who migrate can retain rights in the *lakou* by providing support and assistance to relatives back home. Haitians living in urban centers may also organize living arrangements in a similar pattern.

lougawou: witch who roams the countryside at night in search of victims.

lwa: a *vodou* spirit. Individuals and families may have their own *lwa*. *Lwa* come to their *sevite* (those who serve them) by entering (possession) their body during a religious ceremony. *Lwa* often reside in special places: *mapou* trees, large rocks, streams and waterfalls.

machann: a market woman or a street vendor. They often travel long distances to sell produce grown by their mates and bring back goods for sale at local markets.

manbo: a *vodou* priestess.

manje lè mò: a *vodou* feast in honor of the dead.

manje lwa: a *vodou* feast for one or more *lwa*.

mòn: mountain; hill.

moun: person; human being; someone.
   moun mon: one from the hills; *moun kay*: a member of the family or a close friend; *moun de byen*: a good person; *moun sot*: uneducated individual; *moun eklere*: educated, worldly individual.

Ozetazini: the United States.

plasaj: common-law union which may be broken at any time by either partner.

plase: common-law spouse. A man may have more than one *plase* at a time.

sosyete: an association, a group of people organized for a specific purpose, for example: a *vodou sosyete*, a *konbit sosyete*.

timoun: child.

veve: an intricate symbolic pattern drawn on the ground with corn flour during *vodou* rituals. Each *lwa* has his/her own *veve*.

vodou: a system of values, beliefs, and practices governing social interactons, the relationship between humans and supernaatural beings.

BIBLIOGRAPHY

Allman, James
1982   Haitian Migration: 30 Years Assessed.
          Migration Today 10(1):7-12.

Allman, James and Karen Richman
1985   Migration Decision Making and Policy, the
          Case of Haitian International Migration,
          1971-1984. Paper presented at the Popula-
          tion Association of America Meetings, Bos-
          ton, Massachussets.

Bajeux, Jean-Claude
1973   Les Haitiens en Republique Dominicaine.
          Sel (10):13-20.

Bastide, Roger, F. Morin, and F. Raveau
1974   Les Haitiens en France. The Hague: Mouton.

Bastien, Remy
1961   Haitian Rural Family Organization. Social
          and Economic Studies 10:478-510.

Bateson, Gregory
1972   Steps to an Ecology of Mind. San Fran-
          cisco: Chandler Press.

Beard, John Reilly
1853   The Life of Toussaint Louverture, the Negro
          Patriot of Hayti, Comprising an Account of
          the Struggle for Liberty in the Island, and
          Sketches of its History to the Present
          Period. London: Ingram Cooke.

Berardin-Haldemann, Verena
1972   Femmes Haitiennes a Montreal. These de
          Maitrise, Universite de Montreal.

Berggren, Gretchen, et al.
1980   Haiti's Artibonite Valley: Migration and
          Instability. Migration Today 8(1):13-21.

Bitter, Maurice
1970   Haiti. Paris: Editions du Seuil.

BOCES Geneseo Migrant Center
1984   Migrant Heritage Studies Project, Haitian
          Component. SUNY Geneseo, NY.

Boggio, Philippe
1982   La Guyane Francaise fait face a un afflux
          de refugies haitiens. Le Monde, 4 mai: 10.

Bogre, Michelle
1979   Haitian Refugees: Haiti's Missing Persons.
          Migration Today 8(4):9-10.

Bott, Elizabeth
1971   Family and Social Network.   New York: Free
          Press.

Bryce-Laporte and Roy Simon
1977   The New Immigrant Wave.   Society,
          14(6):18-79. Sept./Oct. (Special Issue)

1978   The New Immigration and its Caribbean Com-
          ponent - an Overview. Testimony before the
          Select Committee on Population. U.S. House
          of Representatives. Washington, D.C.: U.S.
          Government Printing Office.

1979a   New York City and the New Caribbean Im-
          migration: A Contextual Statement.   Inter-
          national Migration Review 13(2): 214-234.

1979b   Sourcebook on the New Migration to the
          United States. New Brunswick, NJ: Transac-
          tion Books.

Bryce-Laporte Roy and Delores Mortimer
1976   Caribbean Immigration to the United States.
          Washington: Smithsonian Institution,
          Research Institute on Immigration and Eth-
          nic Studies (RIIES) Occasional Papers 1.

Buchanan, Susan
1979   Language and Identity Among Haitians in New
          York City.   International Migration Review
          13: 298-313.

1981   Profile of a Haitian Migrant Woman.   In
          Female Immigrants to the United States:
          Caribbean, Latin American, and African Ex-
          periences.   D. M. Mortimer and R. S.
          Bryce-Laporte, eds. RIIES, Occasional
          Papers No.2. Washington, D.C.: Smithsonian
          Institution.

1981b   Haitian Emigration: The Perspective from
           South Florida and Haiti.

1983   The Cultural Meaning of Social Class for
           Haitians in New York City.   Ethnic Groups,
           5:7-30.

Bureau of the American Republics
1893   Haiti.   Bureau of the American Republics:
           Washington, D.C..

Chaney, Elsa M.
1982   Women Who Go...Women Who Stay Behind.
           Migration Today 10(3/4):8-13.

Chierici, Rose-Marie
1985   Haitian Women in the Migrant Stream. Paper
           presented at the 25th Meetings of the NEAA,
           Lake Placid, NY.

1987   Making it to the Center: Migration and
           Adaptation Among Haitian Boat People.   New
           York Folklore, 8(1-2):107-16.   (Special
           Issue: The New Nomads: Arts, Life, and Lore
           of Migrant Workers in New York State).

Chierici, Rose-Marie and Sue Roark-Calnek
1984   Two Models for the Construction of Ex-
           perience Among Haitian Immigrants.   Paper
           presented at the Annual Meeting of the
           American Anthropological Association, Den-
           ver, CO.

Comhaire-Sylvain, S. and J.
1959   Urban Stratification in Haiti.   Journal of
           Social and Economic Studies 8(2):179-189.

Congressional Record-Senate.
1980   Congressional Quarterly Inc., Sept. 25, pp.
           S 13492-13493.

Congressional Quarterly; Law/Judiciary.
1984   Congressional Quarterly Inc., June 23, pp.
           1493-1500.

Corten, Andres, et al.
1976   Azucar y Politica en la Republica
           Dominicana.   Santo Domingo: Ediciones de
           Taller.

Craig, D.
1979   Immortality Through Kinship: the Vertical
           Transmission of Substance and Symbolic Es-
           tate. American Anthropologist 81:94.

Davidson, R.B.
1962   West Indian Migrants: Social and Economic
           Facts of Migration from the West Indies.
           London: Oxford University Press.

Davis, Harold P.
1928   Black Democracy. New York: The Dial Press.
           (1967, Noble Offset Printers, Inc.).

Davis, Wade
1985   The Serpent and the Rainbow. New York:
           Simon and Schuster.

Dejean, Paul
1978   Les Haitiens au Quebec. Montreal: Univer-
           sity Quebec Press.

Department of Health and Human Services.
1983   Memorandum; Revised Chart on Eligibility of
           Aliens for Major Assistance Programs. So-
           cial Security Admininstration, Office of
           Refugee Resettlement, 31 January.

Deren, Maya
1953   Divine Horsemen: The Living Gods of Haiti.
           New York: Chelsea House.

Diaz, Alberto P.
1973   Guanamaca, une communaute Haitienne a Cuba.
           Sel (9):28-37.

Diederich, Bernard and A. Burt
1969   Papa Doc: the Truth about Haiti Today. New
           York: Mc Graw-Hill.

Dominique, Max
1982   Les Haitiens aux Bahamas. Collectif
           Paroles, 16 fevrier/mars: 23-24.

Dominguez, Virginia
1975   From Neighbor to Stranger: the Dilemma of
            Caribbean Peoples in the United States.
            Antilles Research Program, Occasional
            Papers 5. New Haven, CT: Yale University
            Press.

Duarte, Isis, et al.
1976   Immigracion Haitiana y Prodccion Azucarera
            en la Republica Dominicana. Santo Domingo.

Durkheim, Emile
1933   The Division of Labor in Society. London:
            The Free Press.

Elwell, Patricia, et al.
1977   Haitian and Dominican Undocumented Aliens
            in New York City: a Preliminary Report.
            Migration Today 5:5-9.

Epstein, A.L.
1964   Urban Communities in Africa. In Closed
            Systems and Open Minds. M. Gluckman, ed.
            Chicago: Aldine Publishing Company.

Fink, Marcy
1979   A Dominican Harvest of Shame.   Caribbean
            Review 8 (1).

Fontaine, Pierre-Michel
1976   Haitian Immigrants in Boston: a Commentary.
            In Caribbean Immigration to the U.S.
            R. Bryce-Laporte and D. Mortimer, eds.
            RIIES Occasional Papers, No. 1. Washington,
            D.C.: Smithsonian Institution.

Foreign Policy Association - World Affairs Center.
1922   The Seizure of Haiti by the United States,
            a Report on the Military Occupation of the
            Republic of Haiti and the History of the
            Treaty Forced upon Her. Washington, D.C.:
            National Popular Government League.

Fortes, Meyer
1949   Time and Social Structure. In Social
(1970)   Structure and Other Essays. Meyer
            Fortes, ed. pp. 1-20. New York: Athlone
            Press.

1968   Introduction. In The Developmental Cycle
            in Domestic Groups.   Jack Goody, ed.
            Cambridge: Cambridge University Press.

1969   Kinship and the Social Order. Chicago: Al-
            dine Publishing Company.

1971   Some Aspects of Migration and Mobility in
            Ghana.   Journal of Asian and African
            Studies 6(1):1-20.

Francis, Cherie
1984   Haitian Entrant Relocation in Philadelphia-
            Introduction: Relations Among Haitians.
            Paper presented at the 83rd Annual Meeting
            of the American Anthropological Associa-
            tion, Denver, CO.

Genovese, Eugene D.
1979   From Rebellion to Revolution. Baton Rouge:
            Louisiana State University Press.

Glick, Nina
1969   Ethnic Groups and Boundaries. In The So-
            cial Organization of Culture Difference.
            F. Barth, ed. Boston: Little and Brown Co.

1971   The Creation of an Ethnic Group in New York
            City. Paper presented at a meeting of the
            Society for Applied Anthropology.

1975   The Formation of a Haitian Ethnic Group.
            Ph. D. dissertation, Department of
            Anthropology, Columbia University.

Gluckman, Max
1955   Custom and Conflict in Africa. Oxford:
            Basil Blackwell.

Graves, Nancy B. and Theodore D. Graves
1974   Adaptive Strategies in Urban Migration.
            Annual Review of Anthropology, Vol. 3.
            Bernard J. Siegel, Alan Beals and Stephen
            A. Tyler eds. Palo Alto, CA.: Annual
            Reviews Inc.

Green, Vera
1975   Racial Versus Ethnic Factors in Afro-
          Caribbean Migration. In Migration and
          Development: Implications for Ethnic Iden-
          tity and Political Conflict. Paris and The
          Hague: Mouton.

Haitian Centers Council Newsletter.
1985   Vol. II, No.1. Brooklyn, N.Y.

Healy, David
1976   Gunboat Diplomacy in the Wilson Era: the US
          Navy in Haiti, 1915-1916. Madison: Univer-
          sity of Wisconsin Press.

Herskovitz, Melville J.
1937   Life in a Haitian Valley. New York: Alfred
          A Knopf.

Hoffman, Leon-Francois
1984   Francophilia and Cultural Nationalism in
          Haiti. In Haiti - Today and Tomorrow.
          Charles Foster and Albert Valdman, eds.
          New York: University Press of America.

Hurbon, Laennec
1984   La Longue Marche des Exiles Haitiens. In
          Haiti, Briser les Chaines, Chapter 3.
          Lausanne, Switzerland: Editions Pierre-
          Marcel Fauvre.

Jean-Baptiste, Jacqueline
1979   Haitians in Canada. Hall: Canadian Govern-
          ment Publishing Center, Minister of State
          for Multiculturalism.

Johnson, Anastasia Kosar
1983   Community and the Migrant Farmworker, the
          Interface of Farmer, Migrant, and Provider
          in a Western New York Community. Ph.D.
          dissertation, Department of Sociology,
          State University of New York at Buffalo.

Jones, Robert Alun
1986   Emile Durkheim, An Introduction to Four
          Major Works. London: Sage Publications.

BIBLIOGRAPHY

Kritz, Mary M.
1981   International Migration Patterns in the
            Caribbean Basin: an Overview. In Global
            Trends in Migration Theory and Research on
            International Population Movements. Mary
            Kritz, Charles B. Keely and Silvano M.
            Tomasi, eds. pp. 208-33. The Center for
            Migration Studies in New York City, Inc.

Labelle, Micheline
1978   Ideologie de Couleur et Classes Sociales en
            Haiti. Montreal: Les Presses de
            L'Universite de Montreal.

Laguerre, Michel
1978   The Impact of Migration on Haitian Family
            and Household Organization. In Family and
            Kinship in Middle America and the Carib-
            bean. Rene Romer and Arnaud Marks, eds.
            pp. 446-81. Leiden: Department of Carib-
            bean Studies, Royal Institute of Linguis-
            tics and Anthropology; Curacao: University
            of the Netherlands Antilles.

1978b   Ticouloute and his Kinfolk: the Study of a
            Haitian Extended Family. In The Extended
            Family in Black Societies. D.B. Shimkin,
            et al. eds. pp. 407-45. The Hague: Mouton.

1979   The Haitian Niche in New York City. Migra-
            tion Today 7:12-18.

1980   Haitians in the United States. In Harvard
            Encyclopedia of American Ethnic Groups. S.
            Thernstrom, ed. pp. 446-449. Cambridge:
            Harvard University Press.

1982   Urban Life in the Caribbean: a Study of a
            Haitian Urban Community. Cambridge, Mass:
            Schenkman Publishing.

1982b   The Complete Hatiana: A Bibliographic Guide
            to the Scholarly Literature, 1900-1980.
            Millwood, NY: Kraus International Publica-
            tions.

1984   American Odyssey: Americans in New York
            City. Ithaca: Cornell University Press.

Larose, Serge
1978   The Haitian Lakou: Land, Family, and
          Ritual.   In Family and Kinship in Middle
          America and the Caribbean. A.P. Marks and
          R. Romer, eds. Leiden: Royal Institute of
          Linguistics and Anthropology, Curacao:
          University of the Lesser Antilles.

Leger, Abel
1930   Histoire Diplomatique d'Haiti.   Port-au-
          Prince: Imprimerie A. Heraux.

Legerman, Caroline J.
1962   Kin Groups in a Haitian Market. Man 62
          (233):145-9.

Levilain, Guy Viet
1978   Cultural Identity, Negritude, and
          Decolonization: the Haitian Situation in
          the Light of the Socialist Humanism of
          Jacques Ro[u]main and Rene Depestre. New
          York: American Institute for Marxist
          Studies.

Levi-Strauss, Claude
1963   The Structural Study of Myth.   In Struc-
          tural Anthropology. New York: Basic Books
          Inc.

Leyburn, James G.
1966   The Haitian People (rev. ed.). New Haven:
          Yale University Press.

Locher, Uli
1975   The Market System of Port-au-Prince.   In
          Working Papers in Haitian Society and Cul-
          ture. S. Mintz ed. New Haven, CO: An-
          tilles Research Program.   Yale University
          Press.

1984   Migration in Haiti. In Haiti - Today and
          Tomorrow. C.E. Foster and A. Valdman,
          eds., New York: University Press of
          America.

Lofficiel, Frantz
1979   Creole Francais: Une Fausse Querelle.
          Bilinguisme et Reforme de l'Enseignement en
          Haiti.

Logan, Rayford W.
1968   Haiti and the Dominican Republic.   New
          York: Oxford University Press.

Lowenthal, Ira P.
1984   Labor, Sexuality and the Conjugal Contract
          in Rural Haiti. In Haiti - Today and
          Tomorrow, an Interdisciplinary Study.
          Charles R. Foster and Albert Valdman, eds.
          University Press of America.

Lundahl, Mats
1979   Peasants and Poverty, a Study of Haiti.
          New York: St. Martin Press.

1982   A Note on Haitian Migration to Cuba. Cuban
          Studies, 12.

1984   The Roots of Haitian Underdevelopment. In
          Haiti - Today and Tomorrow. C.R. Foster
          and A. Valdman, eds. New York: Lanham.

MacDonald, John S. and Leatrice MacDonald
1964   Chain Migration, Ethnic Neighborhood, and
          Social Networks.   Millbank Memorial Fund
          Quarterly 42:82-97.

Maingot, Anthony P.
1985   The Stress Factors in Migration: a Dissent-
          ing View. Migration Today 13(5):26-32.

Malenfant.
1924   Des Colonies, Particulierement de Celle de
          Saint Domingue. Paris: Audubon.

Marshall, Dawn I.
1979   "The Haitian Problem" Illegal Migration to
          the Bahamas. Kingston (Jamaica): Institute
          of Social and Economic Research, University
          of the West Indies.

1982   The History of Caribbean Migrations: the
          Case of the West Indies. Caribbean Review
          11(1).

Mattera, Gloria and James Watson
1983   Alcohol Use Among Migrant Laborers. Study
          conducted under the supervision of the
          BOCES Geneseo Migrant Center.

Mayer, Philip
1961   Townsmen or Tribesmen.   London: Oxford
          University Press.

Metraux, Alfred
1960   Haiti: Black Peasants and Voodoo.   New
          York: Universe Books.

Metraux, Rhoda
1952   Some Aspects of Hierarchical Structure in
          Haiti.   In Acculturation in the Americas.
          S. Tax, ed. Chicago: University of Chicago
          Press.

Mintz, Sidney
1960   Peasant Markets.   Scientific American
          203(2):112-118.

1969   Internal Market Systems as Mechanisms of
          Social Articulation. American Ethnological
          Society, Proceedings of Spring Meeting.

1966   Introduction to the Second Edition.   The
          Haitian People.   James G. Leyburn pp.
          v-xlii. New Haven: Yale University Press.

1971   Men, Women, and Trade. Comparative Studies
          in Society and History 13:247-261.

Mitchell, J. Clyde
1969   The Concept and Use of Social Networks. In
          Social Networks in Urban Situations. J.C.
          Mitchell, ed. New York: Humanities Press.

Nachman, Steven R.
1984   Employment Services for Haitian Women at
          HACAD, INC. Paper presented at the Haitian
          Women's Conference.

Nachman, Steven R. Susan M. Widmayer et al.
1984   Infant Feeding Practices Among Haitian
          Refugees in South Florida. Paper presented
          at the American Anthropological Association
          83rd Annual Meeting, Denver, CO.

Nemours, General A.
1952   Haiti et la Guerre de l'Independance
          Americaine. Haiti: Editions Henri Des-
          champs.

Nicholls, David
1979   From Dessalines to Duvalier: Race, Colour,
            and National Independence in Haiti.   New
            York: Cambridge University Press.

1985   Haiti in Caribbean Context.   New York: St.
            Martin's Press.

Palmieri, Victor
1980   Cuban-Haitian Fact Sheet.   Migration Today
            8(3).

Parkin, David
1969   Neighbors and Nationals in an African City
            Ward.   Berkeley and Los Angeles: University
            of California Press.

Perusek, Glenn
1984   Haitian Emigration in the Early Twentieth
            Century.   International Migration Review
            18(1):4-18.

Petersen, W.
1958   A General Typology of Migration.   American
            Sociological Review 23(2):256-266.

1977   International Migration.   Annual Review of
            Sociology 4:533-575.

Philpott, Stuart B.
1970   The Implications of Migration for Sending
            Societies: Some Theoretical Considerations.
            In Migration and Anthropology.   Robert F.
            Spencer, ed. pp. 465-76. Proceedings of the
            1970 Annual Spring Meeting of the American
            Ethnological Society.   Seattle: University
            of Washington Press.

1968   Remittances Obligations, Social Networks
            and Choice Among Montserratian Migrants in
            Britain.   Man 3(3):465-476.

Price-Mars, Louis
1928   Ainsi Parla l'Oncle.   Essais d' Eth-
            nographie. Paris: Imprimerie de Compiegne.

Rainsford, Marcus
1805   An Historical Account of the Black Empire
            of Hayti: Comprehending a View of the Prin-
            cipal Transactions in the Revolution of
            Santo Domingo; with its Ancient and Modern
            States. London: Albion Press.

Richman, Karen
1984   From Peasant to Migratory Farmworker:
            Haitian Migrants in U.S. Agriculture. In
            Haitian Migration and Haitian Economy, Cen-
            ter for Latin American Studies, paper #3.
            Gainesville, FL.

Rotberg, Robert I. and Christopher Clague
1971   Haiti: the Politics of Squalor.   Boston:
            Houghton Mifflin Company.

Safa, H.I., and B. du Toit, eds.
1975   Migration, Change and Development: Implica-
            tions for Ethnic Identity and Political
            Conflict. Paris and The Hague: Mouton Pub-
            lishers.

Schneider, David
1980   American Kinship. Chicago: the University
            of Chicago Press.

Smat, Ouilliam (Smart, William)
1973   Eske Kanada se You Paradi Pou Ayisyen?
            Sel. 10 (July): 52-55.

Smith, Patrick Bellegarde
1985   In the Shadow of Powers.   Atlantic High-
            lands, NJ: Humanities Press Internatonal,
            Inc.

Smucker, Glenn R.
1984   The Social Character of Religion in Haiti.
            In Haiti - Today and Tomorrow, an Interdis-
            ciplinary Study. Charles R. Foster and Al-
            bert Valdman, eds.   New York: University
            Press of America.

Souffrant, Claude
1975   La Situation Dramatique de Quelques
            Haitiens a New York. Presence Haitienne 1.

Stack, Carol
1974   All Our Kin: Strategies for Survival in a
         Black Community. New York: Harper and Row.

Stepick, Alex
1982   Haitian Boat People: a Study in the Con-
         flicting Forces Shaping U.S. Immigration
         Policy. Law and Contemporary Problems
         45(2)163-96. Duke University.

1984   The Roots of Haitian Migration. In Haiti -
         Today and Tomorrow, an Interdisciplinary
         Study. Charles R. Foster and Albert
         Valdman, eds.. New York: University Press
         of America.

1984b   Haitians Released from Krome: Their
         Prospects for Adaptation and Integration in
         South Florida. Dialogue #24. Miami: Latin
         American and Caribbean Center, Florida In-
         ternational University.

1984c   The Business Community of Little Haiti.
         Dialogue #34. Miami: Latin American and
         Caribbean Center, Florida International
         University.

Steward, William A.
1968   Distribution of Creole and French in Haiti.
         In Georgetown University Round Table,
         Selected Papers in Linguistics 1961-65.
         R.J. O'Brien, ed. Washington: Georgetown
         University Press.

Sutton, Constance and Susan R. Makiesky
1975   Migration and West Indian Racial and Ethnic
         Consciousness. In Migration and Develop-
         ment: Implications for Ethnic Identity and
         Political Conflict. Helen I. Safa and
         Brian Du Toit. eds.. Paris, The Hague:
         Mouton.

Sutton, Constance
1975   Comments. In Migration and Development:
         Implications for Ethnic Identity and
         Political Conflict. Helen I. Safa and
         Brian Du Toit, eds. pp. 175-85. Paris, The
         Hague: Mouton.

United Nations, ECLA.
1981   Statistical Yearbook for Latin America
            1980. Santiago, Chile: United Nations.

U.S. Department of Justice.
1984   Personal Communication (letter). Community
            Relations Service, Northeast Region. 30
            April.

United States Department of State.
1986   U.S. Assistance to Haiti. Special Report,
            no. 141. Bureau of Public Affairs,
            Washington, D.C.

Valdman, Albert
1984   The Linguistic Situation of Haiti. In
            Haiti - Today and Tomorrow. C.R. Foster
            and A. Valdman, eds.. New York: University
            Press of America.

Van Gennep, Arnold
1960   The Rites of Passage. Chicago: The Univer-
            sity Press of Chicago.

Walsh, Bryan O.
1979   Haitians in Miami. Migration Today 7 (4):
            42-44.

Woldemikael, Tekle M.
1985   Opportunity Versus Constraint: Haitian Im-
            migrants and Racial Ascription. Migration
            Today, 13(4):7-12.

Yamashita, Yuriko
1984   Haitian Migrant Workers in Wayne County, a
            Communication Project. Department of Com-
            munication Arts, Cornell University,
            Ithaca, New York.

INDEX